BY THE SCRUFF OF MY NECK

Dr. Craig W. Fisher

ISBN 978-1-68526-904-3 (Paperback)
ISBN 978-1-68526-906-7 (Hardcover)
ISBN 978-1-68526-905-0 (Digital)

Copyright © 2022 Dr. Craig W. Fisher
All rights reserved
First Edition

All rights reserved. No part of this publication may be reproduced, distributed, or transmitted in any form or by any means, including photocopying, recording, or other electronic or mechanical methods without the prior written permission of the publisher. For permission requests, solicit the publisher via the address below.

Covenant Books
11661 Hwy 707
Murrells Inlet, SC 29576
www.covenantbooks.com

CONTENTS

Acknowledgments v

Chapter 1:   The Move 1
Chapter 2:   The Home 11
Chapter 3:   Routine 18
Chapter 4:   The Lesson Learned 23
Chapter 5:   Foamer and a Dummy 27
Chapter 6:   The Skunk 30
Chapter 7:   Flies and Grounders 33
Chapter 8:   Curly 36
Chapter 9:   The Fight 41
Chapter 10: Fun in the Pasture 45
Chapter 11: Exploration 49
Chapter 12: Visitors 53
Chapter 13: Swimming 57
Chapter 14: The Tracks and the Pier 61
Chapter 15: Mystery Solved 67
Chapter 16: The Turning Point 72
Chapter 17: A New Counselor 75
Chapter 18: The Clubhouse 79
Chapter 19: Baseball 86
    Camp Hollis 86
    Baseball Team 88
Chapter 20: The Closing 93
Chapter 21: Syracuse at Mom's 97
Chapter 22: Syracuse at Pop's 103
Chapter 23: The Two Most Influential People in My
              Early Years 110
    Mr. John 110
    Aunt Bunny 112
Chapter 24: Epilogue 115

ACKNOWLEDGMENTS

This book is a walk-through of true-life adventures that my siblings and I experienced while living in a children's home for six years. My daughter, Pam, and my two sons, Dan and Rob, provided significant inspiration for me to document some of those activities. I'll always hear Pam saying, "What about the time you chased a skunk but it caught you?" On the other hand, it has an underlying theme of some young boys searching for a stable home.

How we survived seems like a miracle to all of us. Psychologists and social workers are pressing for youngsters to be moved into family-oriented care, e.g., foster homes, with the belief that group homes do not adequately support the individual. I'll leave that question to be solved by those experts, but I do suggest that I have seen many youngsters come out of foster homes who have been mistreated. And some caretakers at the home mistreated us. But the deciding factor is not the group environment versus the foster care environment. The deciding factor is the character of the individuals providing the caring environment. Mr. "John" in our life is a perfect example.

Professional writer, Lorraine Hartin-Gelardi, and her writing club at the Millbrook Fountains gave me the courage to continue telling these stories. She is very knowledgeable and talented, but mostly she is extremely kind. I could not have a better mentor.

Several old friends functioned as readers and provided very useful input. I am indebted to them for sticking with me throughout this process. They are Bert and Margie McConnell, Alan and Karen Conover, Ed and Sue Lynch, and Pat Zito.

CHAPTER 1

The Move

It was so blustery that when I took my first step out into the darkness, I lost my balance and tumbled down to my hands and knees. As I got up, the hurricane level 1 wind tried its hardest to knock me down again. Every time I started to lift a foot, my balance was shaken to the core. I took baby steps but still had to walk leaning over sideways. Each move was a struggle, and my shirt was filling up with air, sort of like a hot air balloon raring to fly away. My three older brothers laughed and said, "Just go to the outhouse. Don't be such a baby. Six-year-olds can walk farther than that." It took many minutes as my baby steps were not very sure. I made it there and had to fight the torrential wind and now downpour just to open the door. The door came about five inches open and then *slammed shut* over and over. Finally, after a few more tries, it stayed open long enough for me to climb up on the cold hardwood and sit over the big hole in the board. Then the swirling wind played a dirty trick and blasted the door wide open. I had to do my business with the door wide open and the wind and rain lashing out at me.

As I sat there, I kept asking myself, "Why the h—— did we have to move here? It is miserable. My brothers and sister are miserable. Mother and pop are miserable. We're all miserable. Why leave such a beautiful home with toilets and running water and a bathtub to move to this dump? There is not even a regular school—just a two-room house, one room for grades 1 to 3 and one room for grades

4 to 6. Mother and Pop sure tricked us when they said we were moving to a nice family farm. I'm tired of dirty tricks." How did it all start to go so bad?

I remember Mother telling Pop that we were moving from our home in Syracuse, New York, to Grandpa's farm near Oneida Lake in Oswego County. It made sense to Mother since after her father died, our grandmother Nana and Nana's older sister, Jenny, needed some help managing the farm. The plan was that they could also take care of us, five kids, while Mother and Pop commuted to their jobs in Syracuse.

My sister Christine, a year and a half younger than me, was a cute little blonde who was still five when I turned seven. My three older brothers dwarfed me. My oldest brother, Tom, used to say that I was the runt of the litter. Whatever that meant. Tom was six years older and way up into eighth grade so our paths didn't intersect very much.

The second oldest, Dennis, had attended a special school in Syracuse because he had something wrong with his speech and social skills. Mother said, "He has these problems because he couldn't hear for the first three years of his life. You have to hear in order to learn to talk right."

But he was clever and had a great sense of humor. Once in a while, Dennis would make himself a sandwich but get distracted and work on a game. He was always playing games or something, and Frank would reach around the corner and swipe his sandwich. Frank thought he got away with it, but Dennis knew and planned his revenge. The next time Dennis made himself a sandwich, he flavored it with lots of vinegar. After Frank coughed that up, he didn't take sandwiches from Dennis anymore.

Frank, a year and a half older than me, was very huge and had an adventurous attitude right from the start. Once he stood on the corner of Genesee Street, a very busy thoroughfare in Syracuse, and got on a city bus right behind some lady. He went all the way to the back of the bus. When he didn't show up for lunch, everyone at home was looking for him and, in a panic, calling all the neighbors to see if anyone saw him or knew his whereabouts. No one did.

BY THE SCRUFF OF MY NECK

Several hours later, a man, in a big new car, drove up to the house and knocked on our door with Frank in tow. Mother answered the door.

The man asked, "Is this your boy?"

"Yes, we've been looking for him."

"Well, keep your eye on him. You should always know where your children are going! Don't you keep your eye on them?"

"Of course, but with five kids, it isn't always possible. Who are you to talk like that to me? How did you find Frank?

He then explained, "I'm a bus driver, and as I cleaned up the bus at the end of my route, I found this young guy laid out on the back seats sound asleep. At least he knew his address, I'll give you that. But be more careful in the future as you never know what could happen or who would try to 'befriend' him."

Mother said, "I try to be careful, but with so many kids, it isn't so easy to watch all of them all the time, especially these overactive boys."

"But if you don't, then who will? You are responsible."

"Thank you for bringing him home, but don't lecture me."

The driver left shaking his head.

It seemed like Frank had a calling for adventure—and he would certainly find it.

Later, I asked, "Frank, did she spank you?"

"Yeah, but it didn't hurt. She used her hand and not a stick as she does on Tom."

To get to school, Frank and I walked past a yard that had a dog much bigger than me who always liked to bark at us. Frank said, "It's okay, he's fenced in, and Great Danes are not mean dogs anyway. He's just saying hello." He had a knack for helping underdogs which came in very handy as we grew up in a strange variety of situations.

I loved our school. The kindergarten room was huge and full of colorful puppets, toys, and games. But most of all, the room was full of cheerful kids and two teachers with great big smiles. The kids were not towering over me as my three big brothers did. Philip and Toby became my best friends as the three of us loved to play with Lincoln Logs and a farm set that included miniature cows, sheep, dogs, horses, a large red barn with a green roof, and a white silo. We made fences for the animals and built a farmhouse with the logs. What could be better than that? As much as I liked our Syracuse house, I looked forward with great anticipation to move to a farm.

My first home in Syracuse, New York. Source: unknown.

One morning, my three older brothers were scurrying around, filling boxes and bags. My younger sister, Christine, and I had no idea what was up. "Hey, Frank, what's going on?"

Frank said, "Remember Mother told Pop that we were moving."

"Yes, but I didn't think much about it. What about all my new friends at school?" I loved going to school. And now we have to leave it. "When are we going?"

Frank explained that after Grandpa Loke, our mother's father, died, we could move into that farmhouse with no rent. Besides the money saved, it made sense to Mother since after her father died, our grandmother Nana and her older sister, Jenny, needed some help managing the farm. They could also take care of us, five kids, while Mother and Pop worked in the city. So it was all decided. We are moving from our beautiful bright yellow two-story house in the heart of Syracuse, New York, to grandpa's isolated farm near Oneida Lake in Oswego County. Little did we know how short-lived our stay on the farm would be.

The more I thought about moving to live on a farm, the more excited I became. I have seen pictures of farms with lots of cows and horses in huge fenced-in fields. Visions of men on horseback riding out to fix the fences increased my anticipation. There would be chickens running around the barnyard, cute little pigs in their pens, and lassie-like collie dogs barking and playing. Men would work in the gardens while the women prepared lavish meals. The dream of the aroma of apple and blueberry pies whetted my appetite. What could be greater than moving to a farm? I was all in and couldn't wait for the move to begin. But I noticed that no one else seemed too happy about it all. Soon I would learn why.

The farm. The photo was taken by Frank Fisher in 2012, sixty-plus years after we lived there. The house was restored, the barn in sad shape, and the trees now dwarfed the place. The foreground was the cemetery where our nana was buried.

As we drove onto the muddy and rocky set of parallel paths that was called a driveway, the light of my excitement dimmed. On the side of the driveway, there stood a shabby brown farmhouse with a slanted porch. A big gray garage was a few yards in front of us. I asked, "Where's the giant red barn with a tall white silo?"

Tom blurted out, "Hey, dummy, that's the barn right in front of you."

"That little gray thing? Where is the one to keep all the cows and horses?"

Pop said, "There is only one horse and no cows. We may be getting some pigs and chickens soon."

I saw no fences or gardens either but decided not to ask any more stupid questions.

Nana and Aunt Jenny warmly greeted us as we exploded into the exceptionally large kitchen. All nine of us could easily fit around the mammoth table. The black, heavy-looking wrought iron stove sure kept the kitchen hot enough. There were lots and lots of cupboards but no pictures anywhere that I could see. Next to the overly waxed linoleum floor, everything else seemed pretty crab.

We kids just stood there wondering, *What is this place? Where we would sleep?* The oldest, Tom, was lucky as he got to sleep on a daybed in the living room. He was lucky because it was right next to the kerosene heater that was used for keeping that side of the house warm. Mother and Pop got a room that was on the left of the living room. Nana had a bedroom on one side of the kitchen by the iron stove. Aunt Jenny's room remained a mystery to me. Just beyond the far side of the stove was a doorway leading up some stairs. Christine got her bedroom on one side of the stairs, and Frank and Dennis got a room on the other side of the stairs.

I didn't see a room for me; but just as I started to ask, Pop showed me that by turning right at the top of the stairs, there was another very narrow stairway, about the size of a step ladder, leading up to another bedroom. It was small and very high up. It was built into one side of the attic. Mother said, "You're a big boy now, and you can have your own room."

Tom said, "Hey, where's the bathroom?" Pop took us out a back door through a shed and pointed to a small shack about fifteen yards away. It was an outhouse about the size of two telephone booths. Washing up and baths were never mentioned.

So after living arrangements were all settled, we began just that—living. Mother and Pop had to get up before we did so they could drive to Syracuse where they still worked. We were given a set of chores to do every morning. Nana was especially kind and loving. Frank, the third born, was particularly close to her. Nana was all smiles and full of hugs to give to us. Aunt Jenny was kind of neutral to all of us and was always worried that we might be doing something wrong and getting into trouble.

Tom, the firstborn, and Frank didn't seem to get along very well. I think Frank might have been a threat of some type to Tom, four years younger but almost as big. Frank never backed down from anything, especially his big brother. Sometimes they would fight and even have battles with Tom using a BB gun while Frank depended on a homemade slingshot for defense. Once, Frank got tagged right between the eyes with a BB. Everyone was having crisis fits and hollering meanly at Tom, all saying that he could have put one of Frank's eyes out. Mother started hitting Tom with a stick as thin as a whip when she got home from work. Jenny started having panic attacks. Pop said nothing.

Even though my dream of a beautiful farm was shattered, I always tried to make the best out of every situation. I became preoccupied with trying to make the barn look a little better. One day, I was cleaning up by throwing ugly, old boards out of the hayloft. Frank, one story below me, looked out to see what was going on, and one of my boards found his head. I learned that heads bleed a lot. No doctors or nurses, but our Mother gave him a lot of ice and gave him a few stitches after shaving part of his head. I worriedly said, "Frank, I am so sorry that you got hit, and I'm glad you're okay."

Frank just said, "I know it was an accident. So, forget about it."

One day, Frank and Dennis were roughhousing in the living room and knocked some furniture over. Aunt Jenny told them to stop. A few minutes later, they broke a lamp. Aunt Jenny got mad and said, "Go upstairs and go to your room." And it was only three. "Don't come down until supper."

I went outside by myself and saw them playing outside. I asked, "Hey, how did you guys sneak out here?"

With a big happy grin, Dennis said, "We jumped out the window!"

"What? From your second-story window?"

"Yup." Dennis continued laughing for some time.

Dennis was always trying to find something that he could do better than others. He became very good at all types of board games, but jumping and climbing were high on his list. Dennis climbed sky-high up in the trees until the top branches appeared to be bending to the breaking point. Jenny screamed, "No more tree climbing. Someone's going to get killed." So of course, we set something up just for her. Dennis laid on the ground under a tree, and we poured a whole bottle of catsup over his face and upper body. Jenny almost fainted as she looked out the window in answer to our cries. She left the household a few days later, saying it was all too much for her.

That was okay with us as she complained too much, and we still had our loving Nana. Then beloved Nana got very sick and very weak. She couldn't even roll over by herself. Mother and Pop kept talking about how sick she was getting day after day. Pop said if she doesn't roll over often, she'll get bedsores. It sounded scary, and I never heard of that and asked, "What is bedsore?" Pop tried to give me some college course on it just to prove how much he knew. No comfort in that. A new chore was added to our list. We had to go into her room and roll her over every few hours so that she didn't get those awful bedsores. She was quite heavy and groaned a lot when we pushed her.

Tom noticed and spoke up about hearing Nana screaming in pain. Mother said, "Pop, don't you think we should send her to a hospital?"

He said, "No, because people give up when they are out of their own home and die a lot sooner in a strange atmosphere." For years after that, I wondered, *What good is a hospital then?* Sure enough, even with all of our rolling her over three or four times a day, she died quietly. After she died, Frank was the most heartbroken. He told me, "She was the only one who ever gave me a Christmas present I always wanted—a pair of cap guns in leather holsters." She understood us and loved us very much.

It was a sad day when she was buried right across the street in the local church's cemetery. The house seemed empty and drab now. No one to take care of us. Mother and Pop kept doggedly driving to Syracuse. Tom was the oldest at twelve years old and took the most initiative in getting us up for breakfast, getting our lunches packed, and getting us on the school bus. But we often went to school hungry because there was no milk for our cold cereal. Sometimes we mixed Ovaltine and water to put on the cereal. Our lunches often consisted of mayonnaise or catsup spread between two slices of bread. If we missed the bus, we had to walk 2.5 miles.

Dinner was supposed to be handled by Mother and Pop, but Mother stopped coming home from work with Pop much of the time. We would go two or three days without seeing her. When we asked Pop where she was, he would only say that she was working late. Pop was a very inadequate housekeeper and rarely made any type of supper.

The farm was a flop in less than a year. We didn't harvest anything worthwhile out of the so-called garden. The horse was sold. Chickens didn't live long under our city slicker care. A few pigs were purchased and sold for a loss.

Left to right: no smiles here. Dennis, Frank, Tom, me (Craig), and Chris. This gives an idea of how unhappy we were on the farm.

I wished we stayed in Syracuse because I missed my old house, our school, and many friends. I was sad and became depressed. I often thought, *How could things get any worse?* I was about to find out.

One evening, Mother and Pop announced a family meeting. I asked Frank, "What is a family meeting? We never had one before."

He said, "The whole family gets together and discusses some things."

I asked, "What things?"

He just said, "Come on downstairs and find out."

I started drooling when I saw a couple of plates of food on the kitchen table, sandwiches cut into sharp triangles, pastries, lots of candy, and bottles of soda—a feast.

Mother and Pop kinda looked strangely at each other, started talking at the same time, stopped, and started again. Mother finally said, "Pop, you tell them." Pop told us that we were going to move again. The children were moving to a children's home in Oswego. Then we all started asking questions. Why? When? What's a children's home? Where will Mother and Pop be if this was just for children? We didn't get many answers; but Pop, as usual, tried his best to paint a rosy picture. He excitedly exclaimed, "There will be a lot of kids to play with and three-square meals a day. The school is a regular school only three or four blocks from the home. The home has baseball fields and a basketball court. The playground has many swings, monkey bars, and even horizontal bars. Also, you can play soldiers as the bedroom dormitory looks just like a real army barracks. There will be rows of cots just like in the movies."

Tom shouted, "What are you saying? Is it better to live in a children's home than with your own family?"

Pop stared at all of us. His hesitation was deadly. Then he blurted out, "Well not exactly, but since your mother and I have to work in Syracuse and can't be home regularly, you need a good place to be."

Frank asked, "Are you promising that this is the best solution?"

Pop just stared at all of us. Then he promised that he will try to visit us every couple of weeks. Now it was Mother's turn to be quiet. No promises there. Finally, the answer to the "when" question was a real stunner. The move was tomorrow morning.

CHAPTER 2

The Home

Mother, Pop, and us five kids all squeezed into Pop's car. A few small pieces of luggage were shoved into the trunk. Mother, Pop, and Tom comfortably sat on the front bench seat while the rest of us jammed ourselves into the back seat. I thought the farm was miserable, but this ride was no picnic. Everyone's pushing and shoving.

Finally, we reached Oswego, and Pop found Ellen Street and drove to the top of the hill. It didn't look like any fun children's place to me. It was a large squared-off redbrick building that made a prison appear warm and welcoming. The worn bricks were either dirty or full of moss and half-dead ivy. After going up the steps and entering the front doors, a rugged-looking lady greeted us. Mrs. Dick was a stern older lady with thick white hair and a witchlike hooknose. She was shorter than my brothers but looked as mean as a stepped-on rattlesnake. Nobody crosses her.

She led us down a hallway past an office on the left and a stairway going up. There was a dining room on the right. Just past the stairway, she pointed into the visitors' room and told us to sit down. Then she laid out the laws with Pop saying, "Yes, ma'am, they'll be good." Within twenty minutes or so, our parents left—they must have been in a hurry or something.

Tom said, "Pop was intimidated and just wanted to get out of there. Also, they had to get to work without being too late."

They reminded us to be good but gave no hugs or well wishes. None of us had any memory of affection from them anyway. Next, we continued down the long hallway. Someone met Christine and took her to some area off to our right. She went to the girls' section, and we rarely saw her anymore. Mrs. Dick led us boys through a heavy metal fire door where Mrs. Wyatt greeted us and marched us through a small hallway.

That hallway came to a juncture. We saw a very large playroom on our left. There was a light green concrete floor, a large empty table in the middle, some lonely benches around the edges of the room, a big chair in the far corner, a TV high up staring down at us with a blank screen. I didn't see any toys or games anywhere. The table and benches were all empty. There was a smaller room with glass doors reserved for only a few older boys. The whole place was barren. Later we found that the benches had wooden tops that could be opened, and various toys and games were stored within.

Mrs. Wyatt began giving us a never-ending list of rules. She gave a monologue, "If you use any toys, you must put them back where they belong to avoid being punished. Only Tom, because he is now thirteen years old, can enter the senior's room. Starting tomorrow, you will be given weekly house cleaning chores. And with each new week, there will be a new list posted. Everyone must help keep your home clean and tidy. The TV will only be played on very wet, rainy, or snowy days. The one exception is we will let you watch it after dinner on Sundays. Is this all understood?" After a long silent pause, she said, "Okay, now let's go upstairs."

On the right side from the hallway juncture, there were stairs going up to the bedrooms and some going down to a gym. Halfway down the stairs, there was a landing with a doorway that opened to an outside courtyard. The courtyard was U-shaped and paved with black tar. The northern side of the U contained the kitchen and dining areas; the western side contained the girls' dorm while the boys were on the east side.

She continued, "Here's your bedroom." The upstairs dormitory had three rows of cots and many locker-size individual closets. They could hold two sets of clothes, a shelf for underwear, and a drawer for shoes and socks. A large bathroom had several sinks, three toilets, and a shower room with four showers. I said, "Yea, no more outhouses." The leftmost row of cots was interrupted by an office that doubled as a bedroom for Mrs. Wyatt, the head caretaker. There was another hallway that led to a second caretaker's room and a large linen closet. So far, we weren't too excited about the army barracks attitude that Pop had portrayed. "Furthermore, you always have two sets of clothes, one for school and church and the other for playtime, also one pair of shoes for everything but the gym which requires sneakers." She reviewed general hygiene practices and finally how to line up for mealtimes.

The "home" from the rear showed the girls' side to the left, the kitchen and dining area in the middle, and the boys' side on the right. The view is from the south side looking north across the vegetable garden. The center is the U where deliveries were made to the kitchen. Source: unknown.

Going out through the courtyard, we saw a large vegetable garden, a barn, a root cellar, and far off to the west, a playground with lots of equipment. Beyond that, there were fields for baseball and football.

As life began we found that we would rarely see our sister as the playground was fenced between the boys' and girls' sides. Even the dining room segregated boys from girls. But we got the routine down soon enough—get up in the morning, then do some chores.

Example chores we as follows:

- Making our beds
- Sweeping floors
- Brushing stairs
- Cleaning sinks
- Cleaning toilets
- Washing bathroom floor
- Scrubbing stains off floors and walls
- Hanging up wet equipment
- Washing windows

We always lined up in that small hallway for meals, and then when it was time, the cook's helper opened the door. And we walked in and sat at one of several round tables that held six or eight kids. So far, there were no big adventures or problems but that doesn't imply that they aren't coming soon enough.

One day, in our first week there, as I walked near the small hallway, I saw my first fight by the fire door. But it wasn't much of a fight. One boy was sitting on another boy's chest and pinning his arms with his knees. The boy on top was holding the poor guy's head and banging it against the floor. I couldn't believe it as I stood paralyzed watching the beating. Finally, he said, "Stick around, and you can get some too." I got quite upset and just left the area as quickly as I could. I just wanted to scream, "Pop, this is no fun place to live!"

The second week of life found me getting beat up by another boy. I had no idea why but was happy that it was only fists, and my head remained intact. I had been looking for something to do and started watching a couple of guys play a game. Then without notice, one got up and slugged me. He said, "Mind your own business," and gave me a couple of extra punches to make sure I got the point. I moved away from there quickly.

Another guy named Floyd saw all of this and asked me to join him in some games. There were a lot of games in the benches: Parcheesi, Monopoly, checkers, Trouble, Connect 4, Operation,

BY THE SCRUFF OF MY NECK

Tinkertoys, and chess became our favorites. Over the next few weeks, Floyd and I became fast friends.

In one box, there were no games but lots of books. These caught my attention the most, and I became an avid reader at the early age of eight years. The church Sunday school leader said that the Bible contained a lot of stories of supermen-type people. Now I didn't find that in the Bible, but these were lots of short books telling the Bible stories like Daniel in a lion's den or Samson tearing down a large temple. You gotta love the little guy, the underdog, David beating the giant Goliath with a stone shot from a sling. Joseph and his coat of many colors, Jonah and a whale. There were stories of huge wars between large kingdoms. The story of the slaves running free from Egypt because Moses, with God's help, parted the Red Sea, but then He closed it when the Egyptian army tried to go through. I just loved reading these over and over. These planted enough seeds in me that, much later in life, I learned to rely on them. Floyd liked them also, and we spent a lot of time reading and discussing them.

Floyd said, "Craig, I really wish I was like Samson. Then I could bring this who building down on any troublemakers."

"Well, my favorite is Joseph and his coat of many colors!"

"Why?"

"After his brothers threw him in a hole and abandoned him, God saved him. He became a big leader helping the king of Egypt. He even gave a lot of help to his brothers when they met up again." And on and on it went over the months, Floyd and I discussing these precious books. Yet we continued to get drawn into the home life.

The third week brought my parents back for their first visit. We crowded into the visitors' room and sat for an hour, mostly just looking at each other. Then a boy walked by, and I told everybody that was the boy who beat me up. Pop said nothing, but Mother said, "Why don't you beat him up?" I opened my eyes wide and stared at her. Then as my eyes got wet, I turned my back to everyone. It was another year or so before we saw mother again even though Syracuse was only thirty-six miles away.

Pop was true to his word and tried to visit every couple of weeks. The trouble was that the visits were quite stilted. We boys would be out in the fields playing some game, and the caretaker would call us in to visit Pop. He was waiting in the visitors' room, and he usually came alone. We all sat there for an hour or so looking at each other and the clock. I never thought of anything to say, and neither did anyone else.

Tom, the oldest, was not much involved with us younger ones. Early on, however, he heard me crying late one night when I was supposed to be sleeping. He walked from one end of the dormitory to the other end where the smaller kids were.

He asked me, "What was the matter?"

"I don't know but can't sleep." He got me a little cup of water and sat with me for a few minutes. Then he started to leave and said to me, "Go back to sleep, and if you can't, then just think about some girls." Why would he say that to me? I hated girls.

Sometimes Tom got rides in police cars, but I never knew why he got so lucky to get that special treatment. But by and large, he was one of the big kids, so we didn't see him much. And he got out of the home after only a year or two.

Later we would learn the truth about Dennis's disability. Needless to say, he got picked on a lot at first. But Frank became his defender, and the teasing stopped. Frank was growing fast, and he never backed down from anyone. He was in some bloody fights but would never quit, so he usually won by pure determination and perseverance.

I didn't like fighting. Well, nobody liked it but did get in my share. Unfortunately, I lost more than I won. There was a sort of "city kid versus home kid" mentality, which caused quite a bit of bonding among us, home kids. We tended to go for walks, hikes, bicycle rides, and so forth in groups of three or more. None of us liked walking alone throughout the city.

Once when I was walking alone home from school, a local boy, Randy, hollered over at me, "Hey, Craig, you must like that shirt."

"It's okay. What's it to you?"

"Well, you wore it all day every day for the last week or so. You must love that old shirt."

"So what? Who cares?"

BY THE SCRUFF OF MY NECK

"Why don't you have a clean one? Or at least wash it?"

"Get off my back."

"Make me."

"Okay!" And I started shoving him. He swung at me and hit me in the face. A feeling of sadness and rage washed over me at that instant, and I began swinging as hard as I could. He fell. I said, "Hey Randy, your shirt is dirty." Then I continued walking home. It was just a little fight, so I didn't even mention it to my best friend Floyd. We usually just went out to the field and played catch until supper.

Then at dinnertime, Mrs. Dick, the headmistress of the home, walked into the dining room with that very stern "holier than thou" look on her puss, and everyone stopped breathing. You could hear a pin drop. With our full attention, she said, "Craig, stand up."

I thought, *What was this all about?* And when I stood, I started shaking.

She said, "I received a phone call from a parent who complained that you beat up her son, Randy. What do you have to say about it?"

I stammered, "It would be different if he won the fight." After a long pause and without a word, Mrs. Dick turned around and walked out. Everybody then clapped and cheered. Now I am home.

CHAPTER 3

Routine

Gradually we became acclimated to daily routines, which included getting up, making our beds with hospital corners, getting dressed in our "play" clothes, washing, doing simple chores, lining up for, and eating breakfast. After breakfast, we would change into school clothes and rewash our hands, faces, and brush our teeth. These were followed by walking to a nearby public school, walking home for lunch, and walking back to school after lunch. At the end of the school day, we changed back into our "play" clothes and then had free time until 6:00 p.m. when we lined up for supper. We wore the same two sets of clothes every day for a week.

Every boy had a chore to do and did the same chore every day for a week. Each week, we rotated chores. Weekends varied slightly as we had to wash or scrub floors, stairs, and walls instead of just sweeping or wiping. No jobs on Sundays except go to church. The routine was the same in the summer except some of the chores increased, which included weeding the large vegetable garden.

There were seldom any problems with these routines as boys quickly learned it was wiser to go along, do the chores, and get it over with. No one liked to get hollered at or even punished for skimping on tasks. These simple routines in our lives may have helped us develop work ethics, or at least the caretakers always drilled that into us: "These chores are for your good." Much later in life, my wife was

BY THE SCRUFF OF MY NECK

very surprised that I made such neat hospital corners on our bed. But it, unfortunately, got me the job in our house of chief bed maker.

Caretakers assigned us to specific beds and sent us to bed at various times for each general age group. My first real experience of punishments happened one night. We younger boys had beds nearer the bathroom while older boys had beds at the far end of the dormitory. Their beds seemed better even though they all looked exactly alike. The three tight rows of beds consisted of three-inch mattresses on springs, which were more like chain-link fences. The springs were hooked to narrow metal frames which were held by rounded metal headers and footers.

The younger boys were nearer the bathroom with all its bright lights and running sinks and toilets flushing when the big boys came upstairs after we were asleep, waking us all up again. The bigger boys' beds were at the far end and close to windows and away from the light and noise of the bathroom.

I complained to Floyd, "What is so special about those guys getting the better beds?"

He said, "Yeah, they should sleep near that bathroom."

Bobby jumped in and said, "We should switch beds, get to sleep in the nice beds, and make them sleep down by the toilets."

About five of us agreed. Some were too scared that we would get beat up. "Nah, not if we are already asleep," we said. So Bobby, Johnny, Lyle, Floyd, and I crawled into the big guys' beds. A great commotion ensued later when older guys found their beds already occupied. I had fallen asleep and had forgotten that I was in someone else's bed. Big John Wiltsie grabbed me by the legs and dropped me on the floor. He took a swing, but I crawled under the adjoining bed. Floyd got hit in the face by David while Lyle got smacked by his older brother Dewitt. I hollered out, "Everyone, crawl under the beds, and they won't catch us." But they tried, so we had to sneak across the aisle to a different row of beds. Since chairs were between the beds, the big guys had a hard time coming across to catch us.

Due to the uproar of shouting, laughing, and running around to avoid fights, the caretaker came in armed with his rubber slipper. The infamous rubber slipper was the sole of a large sneaker with the upper canvas cut neatly off. It made a great paddle as many of us found out. My red backside made me uncomfortable sitting for a few days. Mr. Stafford was proud of his ability to maintain discipline and soon became nicknamed Mr. Rubber-Slipper Stafford.

Lyle wanted to get some revenge on those guys, so a few nights later, we short-sheeted those five beds. Short-sheeting is making a bed with just one sheet but folding it so that it appeared to be two sheets. When a person climbed into bed, he quickly found that his feet got stuck in the middle of the bed. Another big ruckus occurred, but I stayed put and pleaded ignorance.

We also had plenty of free time, and we all agreed there was never any boredom. Something as simple as walking to school was not without some fun. There was a huge house but not quite a mansion on the corner where we had to turn to go down the hill to school. Even our young nonmathematical minds knew it was shorter to cut across the mansion's lawn instead of walking to the corner and then making a left on the sidewalk to get to school.

Of course, after ten to fifteen boys do this four times a day, we began to see our tracks. As the tracks deepened to become a muddy path, we found a big sign on the lawn, saying, "Keep off the grass." Naturally and without hesitation, we stopped making that straight path across the lawn. Our path became a loop to get around that big sign. A couple of weeks later, as the loop became darker and muddier, we found a rope with little pieces of cloth, almost like little white flags, stretched from the corner of the house to a stake at the end of his lawn. Now we did find it more fun jumping the rope than the prior easy walking. Soon the snow came, and we went back to staying on the shoveled walk. By spring, all the fun was gone as a four-foot-high wooden fence completely blocked off the lawn.

I never saw the owner of the house, but my imagination built him into a great man. He never hollered at us and never called the home dignitaries, which would get us into serious trouble. He just kept upping the challenge, almost playing with us. I often wondered why he didn't just make a fancy patio block sidewalk path across his yard. I guess he didn't know the rule about paving the cow paths.

BY THE SCRUFF OF MY NECK

We knew the whole affair of crossing his lawn was wrong and not nice to that man and his house. It was the first sort of mischief that I remember getting involved in, but not the last. One step leads to another, and soon one is on the way down a slippery slope. For example, after finding it so easy to cut across the mansion's lawn, we realized that the lawn at our school was twice as wide as the school. It was very easy to cut across the grass. There was an obstacle that consisted of rules and boys with white-striped belts crisscrossing their chests and backs. They were the safety patrols to make sure that no one breaks the rules of walking on the grass. We got chased and shouted at a lot, but without knowing us, they couldn't report us. And we were faster and more athletic than most of them.

On Tuesday morning, they sprung a trap on us and doubled their ranks and surrounded us. Having done this, they believed they had us; but we fought our way through their ranks, leaving several of them with black eyes and bloody noses. That rumble led to my first but not my last visit with the school principal.

My next incident was when my brother Frank, a friend Floyd, and I were playing in the backyard of the school building on a Saturday. We noticed the shed and decided to investigate what was in it. Of course, it was locked, but the screws holding the lock were in bad shape, along with the softwood. So we just pried them off and went inside. "Wow," said Floyd, "this is just what we need." That was true since our home baseball supplies were only a few worn out-fielders' gloves, and our baseballs were all taped up. So we started to gather some gloves and balls just as two policemen greeted us with shouts of "Police, Anyone in here?" Frank and I dropped our stuff and just stood there. Floyd hopped behind a door out of sight.

The cops tried to put the fear of God in us as they drove Frank and me to the police station. They showed us around and asked how we would like to live in those little rooms with the bars for walls? We got interviewed for about an hour, or so it seemed. Then they drove us to the home where we got into some trouble. We had to stand in the hallway with our arms outstretched for about a half hour. It sounds easy, but you can't do it. So we kept getting hollered at to put the arms back up. I never knew what Tom did to get regular rides in police cars, but I was no longer envious of him for it.

Now we were moving down a slippery slope and found more exciting things to do than fighting safety patrols.

CHAPTER 4

The Lesson Learned

I think they tried to inspire us to follow a spiritual path. We got in the habit of saying grace before every meal—morning, noon, and night. We always said, in unison, "God, bless this food and keep us good. For Jesus's sake, amen." Some got in trouble for saying, "Rub-a-dub-dub, thanks for the grub." At bedtime, we kneeled beside our beds and said, "Now I lay me down to sleep. If I should die before I wake, I pray the Lord my soul to take." I used to worry about what is the probability of us dying tonight. And on Sunday mornings, we got up early to get ready for church. The first thing that we did was say the fourth commandment, "Remember the Sabbath day, to keep it holy," which helps us to remember to keep the seventh day holy as it is a day of rest. Most of us joked around about it all. We often paraphrased Scriptures so we could make jokes about them. However, we began remembering them.

On Sunday mornings, we received our clean set of school clothes to use for Sunday school and then for school all week long. After getting as cleaned up as possible and with our clean clothes on, we were given a small donation envelope containing a quarter for us to give to the church as our offering for the week. I imagine the quarters came out of the home's treasury that has been built up over the years through charities and various government social programs and agencies. I have no idea how we were assigned which church to attend. There were four churches (Methodist, Baptist, Presbyterian, and Christ Church) over a three-block area. Most of us went to one of the first three churches while only Ronnie and Clinton went to Christ Church. Frank and I, plus about seven others, went to the Presbyterian church.

A sample of loyalty was already shown in an earlier chapter, when Frank and I were picked up by the police, we made no mention of Floyd hiding behind a door. Even when pressed by these big overly inflated officers in their sharp uniforms with stars on their chests and guns in holsters around their wastes, we remained quiet. "No, sir, no one else with us." "We didn't break in. The lock sort of fell off." "We weren't stealing. We were observing what kind of equipment is in use so we could copy it when we got home."

Another sample occurred at Sunday school of all places. The concept was all kids meet together in a fellowship hall for opening songs, prayers, and an overview of the lesson for the day. After the leader did his thing for twenty minutes, then the kids went to age-appropriate classrooms. The leader started by saying, "It is very open, and feel free to ask any questions!" When he said, "Don't harbor them under your chest where they will eat away at you," he didn't know the home kids. He said, "Get your questions, doubts, and issues all out on the table for a frank discussion." So Frank said okay and started asking questions. To quote a phrase, he was Frank about it.

The rest of us looked at each other, raised our eyebrows high, and looked at each other as if to say, "Here we go!" Frank never backs down from anyone and doesn't pull his punches. Frank started by saying he thought that Jesus was just a great psychologist. How do we know that he didn't hypnotize and mesmerize people? Frank started to let go of everything he had. He wanted explanations for God letting millions of Jews die in gas chambers. Why do newborn babies die? If Jesus was so good at miracles, why was it so generally secretive? After a little song and dance, Frank asked another question, "Don't you think that the body was taken out of the tomb and hidden someplace to make it look like he rose from the dead?"

The poor leader, probably not rigorously trained in the Bible, was getting very upset, and his face was blowing up like a big red balloon. He told Frank that "if you don't have any faith, then why

BY THE SCRUFF OF MY NECK

don't you just get out of here?" When Frank stood up and started walking out, I and six more boys from the home got up and walked out with him.

Floyd said, "Now where should we go? We can't go home yet, or we'll be in real trouble." Floyd was a pretty hardnose kid who didn't mind breaking any rules but always looked for and planned ways to hide the misbehavior. He was one year older than me but the same size. Gradually he became my best friend at the home. Frank thought of the river. We could walk to it easily as it was only a few blocks from the church. On the way, we got a little hungry and opened up the small white envelopes that were supposed to be donated to the church collection plate. We eight went into a small mom-and-pop corner store, and while some boys bought ten-cent apple pies and kept the cashier busy, others of us put soda bottles and cookies under our jackets and walked out without paying.

We hurried down to the river and decided to hide in case the store owner guessed and chased us. Two large bridges crossed the river. We stopped at the one closest to the home and found a way down under the bridge. We were comfortable that this was a great hiding place. We sat down and ate our loot. Johnny, Floyd's younger daredevil brother, noticed the girders and catwalks that both held up the bridge but also provided a walkway used by maintenance engineers to walk across the river studying nuts and bolts to discover what repairs might be needed.

So up we all went. After a while, we got running back and forth on the catwalk over the center of the river. This was so much fun, but we were running out of time. We climbed down and walked home full of excitement and happiness. We promised each other that we'd be back next week when we would have more time. The whole routine became a habit: use donation money to buy some treats, steal other items, and find the catwalks and girders. After a while, we got pretty good at climbing up and down the girders and started playing tag. We crossed across the river, but it wasn't so easy to get down there.

There was an old condemned building that we could jump onto one of the top floors. But we found that the stairwells were missing quite a few stairs. So we climbed back up, crossed back on the catwalks, and got home cleanly—no suspicion of any misdeeds. We switched back and forth between the two different bridges just to explore and have more variety in our fun. After seven or eight weeks of this wonderful routine, we got called into Mrs. Dick's office where she tried to melt us with her stare. Then she handed each of us our get-well cards from the church. She asked, "Just how sick were you? Where did we go rest if we were too sick to go to church but didn't stay home?" We were kind of immune to her stare and words but not to her punishment. Once again, the main hallway was full of eight boys making a gauntlet by standing along the hallway with our hands and arms stretched out wide.

Right after we got excused and were admonished against further breaches of honesty, we met in the playroom. I told our group that I learned something very important today. After several bullshit exclamations, I interrupted and said, "The lesson we learned is that they open and read our mail!"

CHAPTER 5

Foamer and a Dummy

It was already very dark out as we left the YMCA after playing basketball for an hour and then swimming for half an hour. Carrying our wet towels, Floyd, Lyle, Ronnie, and I started walking the mile through the city back to the children's home. It was a boring walk as we had done it many times. Knowing it was October, I asked the group when was Halloween and how soon can we start going Halloweening. Ronnie, the oldest and biggest of us four, told us that Halloween is not for another three weeks. And you can only go Halloweening the night before and the night of Halloween. Ronnie had a kind freckled face and always seemed pretty mellow whenever we started to plot some activities that were outside the norm.

Lyle said, "We can start Halloweening the whole week before Halloween." This was huge because Lyle was usually timid about starting anything new. He'd always go along with something but rarely started anything. He looked pretty strong with big, rounded shoulders like a tough boxer. Even his face appeared to have gone through a few fights. So he got us going. A big discussion full of laughter followed that idea. Finally, we agreed that we could start trick-or-treating right now. Ronnie convinced us that if the people at the doors we knock on say it's too early, we just tell them that everybody starts as soon as October begins.

Floyd said, "Sure, that's all true but we don't have any costumes."

I said, "We can just put our wet towels over our heads and pull them down tight around our faces and look like little orphans." That caused a little laugh right there.

Floyd was all in and said, "Let's put some dirt on our faces, and we can start right now." So for the next half hour, we stopped at about a dozen houses, but for the most part, we were shooed away without much dignity, causing us to laugh hysterically at all the odd and shocked expressions of the homeowners. To be fair, a few people gave us some candy.

Now we were all in a great mood, almost a drug-induced high. And we started planning on what to do to shake up Mrs. Fulmer. She was the very tough woman who was the keeper of the homegirls. Everything about her shouted out Marine sergeant at a boot training camp. That's just what she looked and acted like—stiff back, perfect posture, craggy face, and such a strong voice that the horse out in the pasture got spooked whenever she hollered at us. And that happened regularly, going near the fence to watch and talk to some girls, and out of the blue, we would hear, "Get away from that fence! I'm taking names and reporting you." We couldn't even see her—then we could find her sitting by her window on the second floor of the girl's wing where she watched everything and anything that ever happened. After a while, we started calling her Mrs. Foamer, instead of Fulmer, as she seemed to foam at the mouth as she worked herself into a frantic state hollering at us. She even blew a fair share of spittle as she hollered. That made us laugh even more, and it was something for us to use when we would mock her.

That wonderful night, walking home as if on air, we came up with an idea. We would make a dummy out of old clothes, stuffing, and a mask. We divided up the tasks. Ronnie, who had the most money, would buy a great lifelike mask. Floyd and I would get the old clothes; and we would all gather stuffing like an old newspaper, hay, and more old rags. Lyle said he knew where there was a rope in the barn, and he would get it.

Late Halloween night, we four went to bed with our clothes on. After everyone else was sleeping, we got up and stole down to the gym in the basement of the boy's wing of the home. We stuffed an

BY THE SCRUFF OF MY NECK

undershirt for the head, filled the shirt and pants until they bulged out—almost lifelike. But we ran into a serious problem. We needed belts and strings to tie off the shirt cuffs, the pant legs; and the head and to attach these parts to make a body, the head to be just big enough to be able to hold the mask securely. Ronnie gave us his belt, and Lyle had seen some twine back in the barn. Lyle went out to the barn and found the twine.

"Okay, who's got some scissors?" I asked, and Floyd pulled out his knife, of course.

So with the dummy constructed, we took it and the rope outside and scurried over to the tree nearest the fence and closest to the girls' dormitory. Floyd and I climbed the tree carrying the rope. When we got to the level of the girl's dormitory windows, we pulled the dummy up on the rope. We then tied him on some branches and made sure he was visible with his face was facing toward the girl's dormitory.

The next morning, before we even got up, all hell broke loose. Mrs. Foamer was foaming, and the horse was spooked. She crossed over from the girls' area, went through the linens and clothes storage area, down our hall, and into our dormitory. This was completely unheard of. She woke us all up and even shouted at our head caretaker, Mrs. Wyatt. She hollered that some of the boys had gotten up into a tree and were watching the girls through the windows.

Calmly Mrs. Wyatt did a head count, and we were all accounted for. The bigger boys went out to investigate and came back in with our dummy. Mrs. Foamer insisted that anyone and everyone involved should get the rubber slipper. While none of us would admit it or rat on anyone else, we got caught. We had inadvertently identified ourselves. First, we started looking at each other trying to suppress smiles and then giggles. Finally, we got laughing so hard that we dove under the covers to hide our hysterics. But the laughter was all too obvious. Our smiles lasted for weeks to come and far outweighed the rubber slipper spanking that one single morning. The story lasted for years, and no one questioned who the real dummy was.

29

CHAPTER 6

The Skunk

It all started so simply. Like any other kids, we loved playing games; and we had a lot of kids ready, willing, and able to play almost anything. We were never bored as we could always create something exciting to do. We started with the simplest regular version of playing tag. But it didn't matter who was it to start because that person would simply catch Floyd's youngest brother Roy who was around five years old. By far, he was the smallest of our group. He was very short with a small round head and a high forehead. I couldn't tell if he was going bald or simply that his hair didn't grow in yet. Roy didn't mind being "it" even though he could never catch anyone. He was just glad to be playing. All we had to do was climb up the huge six-inch diameter poles that held the swing setup or climb the monkey bars or even the horizontal bars. No matter, Roy stayed it until we all got tired of watching him run around like he owned the place. He felt good as he had us all treed, so to speak. He owned the playground!

After trying a myriad of other games like kick the can, follow the leader, or hide-and-seek, we finally hit on a game that almost everyone seemed to like the best. One-two-three-slope involved building a team as we went along. It started something like tag but a little rougher. Whoever was it had to catch someone, not just tag him. A catch was defined by holding him while saying "One-two-three-slope, one-two-three-slope, one-two-three-slope." The rough-

BY THE SCRUFF OF MY NECK

ness came in because the person caught would struggle mightily to get free. Fights were not uncommon.

But after the third saying of "One-two-three-slope," the person caught became a member of the catching team. Two smaller boys, as a team acting together, could capture a bigger boy. Of course, the more on the catching team, the faster they could capture almost anyone. This process continued until there was only one left, and that one would be named it to start the next round. My brother Dennis, the tree climber, could almost always win because he would go so high up in a tree no one would venture after him. However, he never wanted to be it, so he would just quit and leave. So the penultimate person caught becomes it. Dennis could brag that he never got caught, but he also did not endear himself to others and eventually stopped playing, period.

Staying completely on the home property, we covered a lot of territory, including the playground, baseball and football fields, horse pasture, and even the barn. Once Johnny Chatraw, Floyd's other younger brother but who was twice as big as Roy, saw a skunk in the pasture and started to chase him. We all called him back and told him not to chase a skunk. Johnny said, "But that's a problem because if we don't chase the skunks out of the pasture, no one will want to play there anymore."

So Floyd, a year and a half older than me but my size, suggested we talk to some of the older boys and ask their advice. Earl, one of the oldest and getting ready to leave the home to join the Coast Guard, was available that day. My brother Frank, Floyd, Johnny, Lyle, Ronnie, and I went and talked to Earl. Dewitt Cobb, Lyle's older brother, and quite a cynical person was there with Earl. Nobody trusted Dewitt. He was unpredictable and mean. Once in a church league basketball game, when the referee called a foul on Dewitt, he set the ball on the court. Just when the referee came over to pick the ball up, Dewitt kicked the ball high up into the bleachers, right out of the referee's touch.

Unfortunately, Dewitt was there, and he gave his advice. And Earl just stayed out of it. Dewitt told us that if we run fast enough and catch the skunk by the tail and lift him into the air, he can't squirt his smelly formula on us. He told us to "go catch those skunks and get them the hell off our property!"

We must have looked stunned. Dewitt said, "What, are you scared or something?"

Almost in unison, we said, "No, no, we ain't scared of nuttin."

Several days later, maybe even a week, we came across a skunk; and sure enough, we all chased him. I didn't know skunks could run so fast, but we were gaining on him. We also felt strength in numbers and did not want to look like a coward to anyone. Nobody wanted Lyle telling his brother that we chickened out. But just as we were closing in, the skunk crossed the street. We stupidly stopped and looked both ways for cars. That split second gave the skunk time to set up his defenses, and he got us all as we resumed our chase across the street.

That horrible dreadful stench wasn't the worst of it. We now had to face the powers that be within the home. We ruined our clothes that had to be burned. We were reminded over and over that clothes don't grow on trees. We smelled and looked like idiots. We got multiple hot showers with a very strong brown soap brought up from the laundry room. But we couldn't hide—the smell lasted many days. And Mr. Stafford got to practice his rubber slipper on us.

With Dewitt laughing like a mean ol' hyena, we learned the meaning of gullibility. But knowing the meaning of it doesn't mean we are cured of it.

CHAPTER 7

Flies and Grounders

Most summers were great. In addition to all of the other games, we played a lot of baseball and summer basketball. Even if we did not have enough for a full baseball game, we found ways to play. Flies and grounders was a game played with three or more people.

A batter would simply toss a ball up and hit it to the field. The fielders would catch it and throw it back in for another hit, repeatedly. A grounder caught was worth one point, and a fly caught was worth three points. When someone got nine points, he would become the batter. Everyone wanted to be the batter. But the more fielders, the harder it was to become a batter. As more kids joined in, sometimes seven or eight, there would be a lot of competition with boys crashing into each other trying to catch the ball.

There were a lot of fights but one memorable one. Gangly Jimmy Galloway was very tall and determined to win at everything. Jimmy would knock into smaller guys even when Jimmy had no chance of catching it just to keep them from catching the ball. One day, Bobby Merkel, a very handsome boy with a mild manner, got mad and pushed Jimmy hard. Jimmy got up and started punching Bobby so hard that Bobby got knocked out cold. Jimmy just stood there, slapping his hands up and down saying, "One down."

Mickey crashed into me in a very unpleasant way. Mickey was shorter than me but very wiry and as mean as a snake. Something I had tried to forget finally dawned on me—Mickey was that mean kid who beat me up my second week at the home. At that time, I felt shocked and alone and quite intimidated by the entire experience. I just wanted to go hide. The following week, I had pointed the kid out to my mother and her last visit there for about six years. No sympathy from her as she said "Why don't you beat him up?"

Well, since then, I have been in a lot of fights. Besides becoming much more athletic through playing rough games, climbing all kinds of poles and bars, one-two-three-slope, long hikes, and so forth, I got used to the idea that a win or a loss of a fight, you always survived to the next day and were friends again without any thought about prior fights. So I took that opportunity to tackle Mickey and thrash him the best I could. After a while, we were both standing and swinging wildly at each other, both with bloody noses. Then Mickey said, "Hey look, our brothers are fighting. Why don't we stop and watch them for a while?" So we did. Frank made a big point of telling me that Mickey said, "Let's watch our brothers fight," was because he was losing our fight and that I should have kept punching him. Mickey and I never fought again and remained friends until he left the children's home. It always seemed funny, actually weird, to me that so many of the boys fought each other regularly but then played like old friends the next day or even later that same day.

At Lyle's turn at bat, he clobbered one to the barbed wire fence that separates the horse pasture from our playing fields. Lyle was one tough-looking dude and got hold of that one. Boy Scout Ronnie Hulett chased it down but didn't throw it back in as required. Ronnie was an extremely pleasant kid with a lightly freckled face. He was bigger than me by two or three inches and about an inch bigger than Lyle. We all started hollering at Ronnie to throw the ball back in, but he and his Boy Scout mind got interested in something. Why, on this very hot and dry July day, would there be a big wet soft spot in the ground right next to the fence? He always liked puzzles, chess, and a lot of outdoor stuff he learned with the Boy Scouts. Some of us almost resented him wearing his merit badges all the time. But for now, we are left with a puzzle.

Frank said that he was hungry, and it was time for supper. We were all so hot and sweaty that we needed to scrub down. They don't

BY THE SCRUFF OF MY NECK

like dirty boys in the dining area. We can work on the puzzle tomorrow. So we went in to wash up for supper. Floyd said, "Hey! Hurry up! This might be our day for bread and milk, so let's not be late," causing us all to laugh hysterically.

The new guy, Raymond, asked, "What the hell was that all about?"

Floyd shot back, "Oh, didn't they tell you? In the summer, we get tall stacks of white bread with a couple of pitchers of milk for supper every week or so. You just tear the bread up into little pieces, put them in a cereal bowl, and add milk and sugar! Very refreshing actually." Raymond did not look convinced.

CHAPTER 8

Curly

After breakfast and chores were done, we all went back out to see if that spot in the ground was still wet. To our delight, it was soaked. One of the smaller boys, Roy, suggested it might be some kind of animal toilet. We all started laughing except Ronnie. He explained that animals don't all go to the same place. They just go wherever they are at the time. Lyle said, "Maybe it is some big pipe that runs underground and sprung a leak."

I said, "But it's in the middle of nowhere! Why would a pipe be running along a baseball field and a horse pasture?"

My brother Frank, both the biggest of us and the most likely to take leadership of any new strange situation, said, "Okay, that's enough guesswork for now. Let's just dig up the soft wet ground and see what we find."

Bobby Merkel was getting worried. He repeated Roy's question and exclaimed, "How do we know that some animals weren't using this spot for a urinal?"

Ronnie shot back, "Wild animals don't work that way. So let's get started!" Floyd and I snuck into the tool shed in the barn and brought back two shovels. We all took turns digging until we had a hole about two feet deep and a three-foot diameter. To our amazement, the hole was full of water and even overflowing. Ronnie was the first to say that it was an underground spring.

36

BY THE SCRUFF OF MY NECK

One of the youngest, Billy, exclaimed, "Yea, let's make a swimming pool."

He was so excited but got a little depressed when we all said that it wasn't practical. Frank said, "Well, there is a pond in the pasture at the bottom of the hill. It is getting shallow now and always dries up in August. Let's dig a ditch from here down to the pond. It's only a hundred yards or so, and it's downhill. With all of us working together and taking turns, we should be done soon enough. That spring water might keep the pond full of water."

Everyone thought it was a great idea; and we gathered several more tools, hoes, spades, garden hand trowels, and whatever else we could get our hands on, even knives. Frank said, "We can't all work in the same spot, so spread out in a straight line down the hill. We'll each dig sections, and when they all connect, we'll have our famous home boys canal!"

"Yea," we all shouted out. We got busy.

Frank took the softest dirt but hardest part since he had to go under the barbwire fence that surrounded the pasture. As he started, digging he got the water moving, and he was always working in the mud. I was about halfway down the hill digging my leg of the trench. Two or three boys were both above me and below me. I ran into a big rock and didn't know if I should go around it or dig it out of there. I decided to dig it out so I didn't look weak and that my section stayed straight. But it was hard, and when it finally rolled out, it left me with a big hole in the line. Then Johnny shouted some swear words at me as my rock rolled down next to him.

Overall the digging wasn't as easy as we expected. The pasture grass was deep and full of bugs. We also saw several green grass snakes and garter snakes, which gave us some good ideas for later. A couple of the smaller kids dropped out. It wasn't so much fun after all.

Now we are learning a real lesson about the best-laid plans of men. Some of us were digging several inches deeper than others, some a few inches wider, some removing rocks, and others going in looping curves around rocks. But the worst part which made Frank the maddest was that canal sections were not lining up to meet nicely. Now he made us either start over or, when possible, make connections from one section to another. Sometimes this meant east-west sections when the overall goal had been a straight north-south line. Accidentally on purpose, Johnny was tossing dirt out of his ditch into other's ditches and sometimes right on the other boys.

One other major problem was that the ground very quickly soaked up the water that was supposed to run through the one-hundred-yard canal down to the pond. The water didn't make ten yards. We tried everything that we knew, but that wasn't much. We never lived around any adults who could or would give us guidance on these sorts of projects. Our main effort was to stomp and hammer the inside of the ditch to make it harder for the water to soak in very much.

Our only real success so far was getting pretty darn dirty. We finally gave up and got most of the tools put back, not all of them. We were muddy, and most of us tore some parts of our clothing. When we got back home, we tried to sneak in unnoticed, but that was a foolish attempt. The caretakers were watchers and observers and gave us holy hell for tramping all that mud into the building. We had to go take showers, then come down and sweep dirt and scrub floors.

Mrs. Wyatt quizzed us for a long time, finally finding out exactly what we were up to. Usually a very mild, even-tempered woman, but she got mad.

Looking at us in disgust, she asked, "Don't you know that digging holes and ditches in a horse pasture can cause a horse to stumble and maybe break a leg?"

I said, "No, we thought horses can travel any ground avoiding all holes and rocks." Speaking out was my mistake.

She said, "You all have to stand in the hallway with your arms held out level for fifteen minutes. But, Craig, you can do it for twenty minutes for talking back to me."

While the home boys canal was a big failure, we expanded our environment beyond the normal ball fields and playground to include the pasture. We even began seeing the horse, Curly, often. We found out he likes apples, but of course, we got in trouble for feeding him too many apples. But we kept doing it. Now whenever we went up to the fence, Curly would come over for us to pet him and feed apples to him.

Curly came to the fence to meet us as he knew he would get some apples. Here, Jim Condon, Bobby Potter, Lyle Cobb, and Johnny Chatraw pose by Curly as he reaches his head over the fence hoping for apples. Photo by Craig Fisher.

If we could only ride him like a real cowboy or an Indian, that would be so much fun. Talking to some older boys, we were happy to learn how to do it. They said, "It takes four boys to do it right." They taught us that if one boy holds one ear very tight and another boy the other ear that the horse won't buck. So Floyd, Lyle, Johnny, and I brought apples over to Curly. After feeding him, we discussed who does what. I held the left ear and Floyd the right ear. Lyle made a human bench by getting down on his hands and knees. Johnny, the lightest of us all, stepped on Lyle's back and jumped up on Curly's back. Curly immediately bucked, throwing Johnny for a loop. Curly then came down hard, his hooves just missing Lyle by inches. Floyd was safe, but something not so nice happened to me.

Curly's mouth came down over my left shoulder, and he bit me hard. I had tooth marks for weeks on the front and back of my shoulder. Luckily we stopped the bleeding with dirty tee shirts, and we never dared to report it to the caretakers. We didn't want to stand with our arms outstretched for several minutes or worse get a rubber slipper.

The pasture, the pond, a woodsy section in one corner, and the great hill became part of our lives. And we all remained friends with Curly.

CHAPTER 9

The Fight

Caretaker Stafford observed that there were lots of fights between us boys. To us, fighting was never a crisis as by the next day or even the same day the contestants began playing together again as if nothing happened. In school, I learned that animals have a pecking order, and I often wondered if that was what we were going about—establishing our pecking order.

In any case, Mr. Stafford knew that boxing was a great sport. So one day, he showed up with four sets of boxing gloves that he somehow convinced Mrs. Wyatt, head caretaker of the boys, would be an exciting activity for us. Stafford proposed, "The boys will gain respect for the sport while learning how to defend themselves." We all liked the idea as we just imagined ourselves becoming much better fighters, period. Lyle said, "Who just wants to defend himself? We want to learn anything that helps us hit harder and batter the other guy."

Stafford announced his plan to us and invited us to go down to the basement gymnasium. About eight kids joined in this activity. The gym was right under the first-floor playroom and about the same size. At one end were a basketball hoop and net while there was a stage at the other end. The stage wasn't used very much, but once in a while, one of the caretakers would have us put on a short play and pretend that we are all happy at a party. I only remember two plays during my six years at the home. The basketball hoop was very popular and used all year long.

The gym had plenty of room for what he had in mind. He taught us some very basic principles. We lined up side by side with a foot or so between us. "The first thing to learn," he said loudly to get our attention, "is how to stand."

Most of us started laughing as Floyd blurted out, "We know how to stand. We're standing right now."

Stafford shot back quickly, "Your punches will be much harder if you take a proper boxing stance. And you won't get hit as much." He explained that bending your knees a little will make it easier to dodge punches and help you to spring forward as you punch your opponent, giving your punches more power. He told us to stand at a slight angle so that we can lead with straight punches called jabs. Stafford taught, "The jabs keep your opponent away and allow you to set up a much harder punch with your other hand. This opposite hand could be a right hook or a right uppercut or even another straight punch."

"Trust me," he said. "Start practicing these moves so that they become automatic, and you'll win more fights."

Frank made us laugh again as he said, "I don't lose any fights now."

After an hour or so of practicing by ourselves, we quit for the day. He said, "Practice these all week, and we'll have some actual boxing inside a ring next week."

The week went by with us all joking around about who is going to jab who or you better watch out for my upper cuts. Then we came into the gym and saw Mr. Stafford putting chairs around in a square formation with the backs facing the inside of the square even though it is called a ring. After a quick review of last week's moves, he lined us up by height. And he paired us off one versus two, three versus four, and so forth. The plan was to box three two-minute rounds with stress on using all the new moves he taught. The first few matches went as expected, then my turn came. Unfortunately, Lyle was next in line with me, and we got paired off. Lyle said, "You are going to get it now, Craig."

BY THE SCRUFF OF MY NECK

I was trying to follow instructions, but Lyle kept hitting me pretty hard. At the end of the first round, Mr. Stafford called, "Craig, come here so I can tighten your glove laces." But when I got there, he whispered, "Do you want to stop now? It is okay if you quit."

That bothered me, and I exclaimed, "No."

During the next minute, I unleashed anger-driven power that I never knew I had within me. I forgot all the fancy moves and just punched and punched and punched. To everyone's amazement, Lyle quit and said he had enough. The funny thing was I could hardly remember any of the match, and now I am the winner. I beat Lyle of all people.

The bad news was that it went to my head. I felt like a big shot now. Since I am now such a good fighter, I thought about Ronnie.

Ronnie was a very successful Boy Scout. The one scout meeting I ever went to was with Ronnie. He dressed up in his full uniform with a sash half full of merit badges flung at an angle over his chest from one shoulder down to the opposite hip. I wore the same dirty clothes that covered my body every day for the last week. Most of the other scouts were dressed exactly like Ronnie. In the meeting, they were all talking about the big two-week-long scout camp called a jamboree coming up this summer. They could earn three or four merit badges every single day. And it only cost around $250 to attend. That was way over the top for me, and some jealousy was brewing in me, causing me to resent him.

During a basketball game the following week, I started bumping into Ronnie a lot. With no response, I let my elbows fly at his rib cage and shoved him.

Finally, he shouted at me, "What the hell is wrong with you?"

I said, "Nothing, can't you take it?"

"Just stop it."

I boasted back, "Make me."

"No, just stop it, and play fair."

"Can't you make me? Why, are you afraid of me?"

"Not at all, but as soon as I hit you, your brother will come over and pound on me."

I looked at Frank and made him promise not to interfere.

I said in a very cocky tone, "This is just between me and Ronnie, and besides I am going to bust him up."

Frank said, "Okay, you're on your own. Ronnie, I promise to stay out of it."

So we started fighting, but within a couple of minutes, I cried out, "Hey, I can't see." I covered both of my sore well-blackened eyes with my hands.

Frank jumped up, hollering, "What? You can't see?" Then he ran over and pummeled Ronnie.

But I came to my senses and stepped in between them and exclaimed, "Frank, you promised you wouldn't butt in!"

Frank simply replied, "Yeah, but that was before you couldn't see." A few minutes later, we were all shooting baskets on the basketball court.

Floyd came in and asked, "What happened? You look like a raccoon!" Other boys joined in the fun of mocking me.

My head reduced itself back to normal size. To make sure my head didn't get too big again, I carried two big shiners around for the next couple of weeks as a bitter reminder.

CHAPTER 10

Fun in the Pasture

After playing on the playground and ball fields for a couple of years, we needed to start expanding our horizons. Now that we were such good friends with Curly, we started playing in his pasture, which offered a lot. The southwest corner contained a pond, and the southeast corner contained a nice woodsy area. The northeast corner contained a barn with farm equipment and a huge pile of hay. The northwest corner and all the rest was where the grass grew out of control. On sight, Curly always came looking for apple handouts, which we were ready to oblige. The pasture hill was steep, but since it went downhill away from the home, we were very happy to play where we were not seen. In the spring, summer, and fall, we played tag, one-two-three-slope, follow the leader, and hide-and-seek in the tall grass, also played Davy Crockett and Cowboys and Indians.

Today the game was follow the leader. In the past, this game had become pretty routine with things like climbing the monkey bars and jumping off, climbing the poles for the swings, going across the top bar and sliding down the other side, and the like. But today would be different. Daredevil Johnny was small but unafraid to try anything. When he picked the short straw to become the leader, we all groaned. We usually had from five to eight boys in the pack. Johnny led us across the barbed wire fence by crawling under it on his belly, then led us rolling down the hill toward the muddy pond.

Ronnie shouted, "Are you crazy or something?"

Johnny said, "You are either in, or you are out. Don't hold us back. This is still the easy part." Johnny successfully got us all nice and muddy.

Next, we ran along the southern barbed wire fence crossing over the fence and back several times until we got to the trees. Once we got into the woods, we climbed up one tree, went out on a limb, and reached over to another tree to climb down. Then we ran uphill to the barn. Following Johnny, we climbed the ladder to the hayloft that overlooked the pile of hay. He jumped the twelve feet down to the top of the hay pile. We had to follow or get called chicken. It was better to jump early and quickly as the pile got matted down and started to look very muddy and brownish. The smell of it convinced us it wasn't mud. We hurried back to the U patio that had an outdoor faucet and hose to wash off as much dirt and horse manure as possible.

Before the pond dried up, we made lots of little boats and played racing games with them. It was never swimmable. The pond, even as it started to dry up, was the main attraction. We caught numerous frogs, pollywogs, and snakes. The snakes got nice and fat on the plentiful food hopping around. Lyle started digging a big pit, and everyone helped him. He said, "Now let's collect as many snakes as we can and fill the pit with them. Then we'll put Johnny in it." Johnny didn't resist. Lyle's attempt to get back at Johnny failed as Johnny seemed to enjoy grabbing snakes and tossing them out at us. There was never a dull moment.

Lyle suggested that we eat frog legs for a snack. Since Frank and Bobby had matches, we agreed. Ronnie said, "Okay, go grab a bunch of little twigs and sticks." He showed us how to build a small Lincoln-Log type of wooden structure which we set on fire starting with kindling wood. Using our pocket knives, we killed frogs and cut off their legs. Next, we stuck small sticks in the top open part of the legs and held them over the fire. Overall, this venture was not very successful. The legs either burned up on the dry twigs that were

BY THE SCRUFF OF MY NECK

supposed to hold them, or we got so little food out of them that we gave up. As summer drew to a close, we needed something new to do.

The pasture provided a nice wintry playground. Through donations, the home had gathered sleds and ice skates. The pond was shallow enough to freeze early and stay frozen most of the cold Oswego winters. We shoveled it off regularly and had a great time ice skating.

The hill was great for sledding, but we had to work to pack the snow hard enough. Our sleds were the old-fashioned wooden ones with red runners on the bottom. They just dug in if the snow was too soft, but we could pack the snow down. And then the sleds flew down the hill. Ronnie complained, "We go so fast that we either hit the barbed wire fence or have to fall off our sled early."

I suggested, "We get a strong rope and loop it tight vertically to raise the lower barbed wire so we can slide under it." This was immediately agreed upon. Floyd knew exactly where to get some rope out of the barn. Floyd tied the bottom barbed wire to the top one and pulled it very tight. This provided a loop under the barbed wire just big enough for one to slide safely through.

After many uneventful but fun trips sliding down the hill, Frank wanted to up the excitement. "Let's race two sleds at a time. The first one goes under the fence, and the second has to roll over as before." The trouble is that we all had the same style sleds in the same condition, and most were equally fast. I was willing to go against Floyd for the first turn. He won, and I had to roll over in the snow before hitting the fence. Others followed with expected results. No one could beat Frank as he always got a great running dive with his sled. We raced like this for hours.

Then I got paired up with my best friend Floyd again. I kept telling myself, "I am not going to lose again. I've got to win!" We were neck and neck right up to the fence, but just like in playing chicken, we both were determined not to be the chicken. We hit the fence at the same time with neither of us going through the target loophole. A spike of barbed wire gave me a huge cut and almost took my eyebrow off. I bled like a stuffed pig. Fortunately, it did not hit my eye. We also had a lot of ice-cold snow that we kept packing around it. There was no way we were going to tell the caretakers. We just imagined them saying, "What, you deliberately tried to break the fence by pulling it up tight out of its normal position? For goodness sake, you'll pop the nails, and Curly will get out. Go stand in the hall with your arms stretched out wide for fifteen minutes," or worse.

We snuck back into the home, washed up, found some Band-Aids, and lined up for dinner, just another quiet day at the children's home.

CHAPTER 11

Exploration

One summer morning, as I looked south down the road, the same one we chased a skunk across, I noticed that it came to a rather abrupt end. All types of bushes and small trees made a natural fence, but because it was downhill past Curly's pasture, I could see over the thicket. Beyond were green hills and more brush.

"Hey, guys," I called. "What do you think is beyond this road? Has anyone ever walked through that growth?"

"Not me" was put forward by most everyone.

So without hesitation, Frank said, "Let's go." And the first of many regular hikes started that very moment. Our ages ranged from eight to thirteen, and no adult at the home had any idea of where we were or where we were going. I felt elated to start an adventure free from their watchful eyes.

Frank and one of his closest friends, Bobby Potter, took the lead. Ronnie was next in line, followed by Lyle and Johnny. Floyd and I brought up the rear. "You can't go this time, maybe another time after we find out what we might run into," Frank said to Roy and Billy.

As we started hiking through the dense growth, Floyd hollered at his younger brother, telling Johnny to "stop snapping the branches of every bush in our faces. It hurts you know." Ronnie was going on and on about all the different types of bushes we were pushing through. He was so excited exclaiming, "I can earn a lot of merit badges by identifying everything and bringing back samples."

"Yeah, yeah, yeah," we all chorused.

The terrain got muddier as it leveled out at the bottom of the hill. We entered a cove of very tall skinny plants, not bushes mind you, and not trees. I thought that they looked like brown fuzzy fat hotdogs at the top of most of them. Ronnie said, "The plants are cattails which grow in very wet areas. And we can cut the tops off, dry them out, and make torches." It sounded good, so we all started cutting or breaking the tops off. Ronnie told us to leave a long stem on so we'll have a handle to hold onto when we light the torches.

The mud was turning into water, and our feet were getting soaked. Frank said, "It looks like we are going through a small marsh."

Bobby said, "I don't see any way around it."

Most weren't worried about it, and Lyle said, "We've been wet before."

I said, "Yeah, but not in a muddy swamp." Soon all kinds of gnats and bugs were biting us.

In the 1950s, nobody, especially us, carried around fancy insect sprays. Lyle said, "Damn it," and was slapping his face and arms.

Frank said, "Just keep moving, and we'll be outta here soon." Floyd and I didn't like the bugs either but didn't see any danger and could put up with them.

"A lot better than bees," I said.

After about thirty-five minutes, the land dried up, and we could see railroad tracks. "Hey, look," said Floyd, "there are some train cars just sitting on the tracks. Let's check them out." Frank and Bobby started making a big pile of rocks and sticks to be a marker for finding the spot where we crossed out of the swamp going over to the tracks. We all joined in and built an admirable tower of twigs, branches, rocks, and our cattails. I had never been that close to a train before and found it was fun going over to the train cars. Just trying to walk on the tracks without falling off was a new challenge. We walked tight rope style. We ran, which I found easier, and raced. We counted about six train cars. As soon as we got near them, Johnny started climbing up the ladder on the side of the first car. Then we

BY THE SCRUFF OF MY NECK

all followed suit. We sat on the edges of the top of the cars with our feet hanging down inside the cars. Floyd looked further down the tracks and noticed a shack. Floyd and I vowed to go over and look at it when we finished here.

The cars were empty coal cars but full of black coal dust. It didn't take long before we were all covered with soot. We didn't go down inside the cars, but just sitting and hanging around the edges, our hands got black. And every move transferred it to our clothes and faces. Our pants and shoes were very black from sitting, hanging our feet into the cars. This turned out to be such a great day. We played around there for hours. Then a man from the shack came running down the side of the tracks, shouting for us to get out of there. Lyle asked, "Who is he to be telling us to get out of here? Maybe the six of us could gang up on him." Then we saw another man come out of the shack. Most of us didn't want some trouble after such a great day.

With a lot of hilarious laughter, we rushed outta there. By the time we got back to our magnificent marker, it was late in the afternoon. We hurried north splashing through the marsh. Most of us forgot to pick up the cattails that we had dropped in our marker tower. We knew Ronnie kept a lot of cattails in his "always be prepared" scout knapsack and that he would share.

On the way home, I tried some swamp water to help rinse the coal dust off but not with much success. The smell was not appealing at all. When we got home, the caretaker on duty wanted a full explanation for all the black faces, hands, necks, clothes, and shoes. Nobody said a word. We needed to wash up, get some clean clothes on, and line up for supper. A miracle happened—no punishment this time because that caretaker wanted to get us into dinner on time, and then his shift got over.

Our adventure today gave us a lot to look forward to, and we talked late into the night. Floyd asked me, "Who were those two men who chased us?"

I said, "Maybe they were bums living in that old beat-up shack."

Frank put his two cents in since he already had more experience than the rest of us put together. He suggested that "they were probably railroad detectives and used the shack as a makeshift office."

Bobby said, "Yeah, we have to go back there and see what their setup is and what they got that we could use." Many more ideas were batted around for future hikes.

I said, "I want to follow the tracks north toward Lake Ontario. Let's see where it goes." We drifted off to sleep with big smiles on our faces and in our eyes. It was one of our best days of the summer.

CHAPTER 12

Visitors

Mother did not have to keep her word as she made no promises or apologies. After the first three weeks, we only saw her once more over the next six years. That was when she had to come for a court hearing about Frank. And I only saw her at that time for about fifteen minutes.

As passive as Pop was in the early years, under her demanding ways, he kept his word. He had said, "I will try to visit you every two weeks." And he did. Sometimes during bad weather, he would miss a week but kept his word. That doesn't imply that they were great visits. I mean bringing four boys and one girl who were playing with their friends so we could sit around a visitor's room for one hour was not exactly a picnic. "How are you today?" "Did you have a good week?" Around the room, one by one, we were all supposed to give some response.

We didn't tell him things like, "Oh, we skipped church for six weeks and got into trouble," or, "We climbed on the catwalks and girders under the bridges over the Oswego River," or, "We got chased by railroad men for climbing on coal cars," or, "We took soda and pies from mom-and-pop grocery stores without paying." No, we didn't say any of that. We said, "Fine." And we watched the clock tick away the hour, marking the time when we could go back out and play.

Frank and I talked about those visits and did agree that it was admirable for Pop to make the thirty-six-mile trip from Syracuse, through Fulton to Oswego just to see us. This did give us some connection and interest in family roots. Nobody ever asked about mother or spoke about her in any way.

We also agreed that the long visits in the conference room sure messed up our baseball games for two of the better players to have to come inside and sit for an hour. Frank was, by far, the best pitcher on our team, and I was the only catcher. So often, the games just stopped for an hour.

The most incredible visitor was our father's sister Bernice (Aunt Bunny). She flew from Chicago to Syracuse once or twice a year to visit. Pop drove her up to Oswego for her visits. She added a whole new dimension to our time. She insisted we go out for drives. She took us to playgrounds on the river, and we all got out and played catch. Once she brought a bunch of hula hoops, and we laughed and laughed as we all tried to move so they wouldn't fall to the ground. We went over to Lake Ontario to Rudy's and ate hotdogs while imagining that we could see Canada across the lake. She also did not stick to the one-hour-visit idea. She often kept us out for three hours. She blessed us for the rest of our lives. She was the best visitor we ever had.

We were full of smiles on the front step at the children's home when Aunt Bunny visited us. First row: me, Chris. Second row: Aunt Bunny, Frank, Dennis.

BY THE SCRUFF OF MY NECK

We had a variety of other infrequent visitors as well. Some were great, and some were demeaning and condescending. We visited local organizations like the Knights of Columbus (K of C), Elks Club, and Rotary club around Christmastime. Men from the local fire department always came with lots of Christmas gifts well wrapped and marked with labels like "boy 5–7 years, boy 8–10 years," and so forth. We sang Christmas Carols and ate cookies.

The K of C and Rotary clubs brought us to their buildings and gave us meals, sang songs, and insulted us with their pocket-change game. After clearing all the tables off the floor and lining the chairs along the side of the dining room, the men would start throwing bunches of coins around the floor, and we were told to keep whatever we can pick up. We all did it because we wanted the money, but most of us discussed how awkward it made us feel to scramble around on our hands and knees while the men tossed coins and laughed while we chased nickels and dimes.

Having saved up some coins and receiving some Christmas presents with model airplanes and ships, I began a hobby of building models. Whatever money that I could scrape up and save went into this hobby. A most annoying visitor came from the United Fund organization along with a local politician. They came for a photo op. I thought they came to visit, and I was happy that they admired my humble set of models. She asked, "Do you mind if I take some pictures of you and your models?"

I, with a big grin on my face, said, "Sure." She took some pictures telling me how to hold a plane up near my face.

The next day's *Oswego Palladian Times* carried a large picture of me and my model on the front page of the second section. The headline was to the effect that the United Fund had a big part in helping this poor child obtain and build a model airplane. The politician was standing next to me holding up a big Red Feather with the caption "Support your United Fund."

Another type of visitor entirely was the "foster parents to be." Every several months or so, we had visitors work through our playroom and look at us and talk to us. Then a day or two later, one of us (never any of me or my brothers) would get picked to go live with someone for a trial. Bobby Merkel got picked a lot. He was a very handsome boy with thick shiny hair. Being soft-spoken, he made a great impression. But we all knew him better. He was one of us! We took bets on how soon he would be returned to the flock. And he always did.

CHAPTER 13

Swimming

"Relax!" the man shouted in frustration as seven-year-old Peter was as stiff as a board made from a hickory tree. The more the man demanded relaxation, the more that hickory board became petrified wood. Some of the boys began calling Peter chicken. My heart went out to him, and my eyes were watering up just watching him become more and more terrified.

Being new to the home, Peter didn't have the experience of playing in the water with us all summer long. We were all playing in creeks, swimming holes, the Oswego River, and even the shores of Lake Ontario. We even went to glorious Camp Hollis on Lake Ontario every summer for two weeks. That was free due to charity money raised by social services.

Hiking from one end to the other of "three-mile creek" was a great adventure. We always walked in the water up to our knees. Getting some sort of bloodsuckers clinging to our legs was a most aggravating type of incidence. Floyd shouted, "Hey, what are these things sticking to my legs? I can't even pull them off!"

Johnny yelled, "Me too! What are these? Little monsters or something?"

Frank and Lyle stayed pretty calm and said, "They won't drink too much blood, and then they'll fall off when they are full!"

"No, I went them off now. I hate the thought of something drinking my blood," I said.

Ronnie took over and asked, "How many of you have jack knives or pocket knives? If you have them, start scraping those bloodsuckers off."

Roy and Billy didn't have knives and wanted more help. I pulled out my jackknife and went over to help cut those buggers off. But both said, "We don't want you cutting us."

Frank and Bobby had a good idea. They each had boxes of matches in their shirt pockets. Frank lit a match and touched it to the back of a bloodsucker on Billy's leg. Billy said, "Hey, that worked! Thanks a lot." So Frank and Bobby became the heroes and helped everyone get the damn suckers off. However, we were all left with red, black, and blue welts where the suckers had been attached. The main point was we were in the water for hours up to our knees but playing and splashing for the pure joy of it all. Some even slipped and fell, getting completely wet. We all just laughed and laughed.

The most dangerous incident, although most of us didn't realize it at the time, happened midmorning. Bobby Potter was taking a turn in front and noticed a snake in the water—but this was different! It was over three feet long.

He started exclaiming loudly, "Hey, a real big snake is in the way."

Frank said, "Take your big walking stick and toss him out of the water onto the ground." Bobby tried. He reached his stick under the long body of the snake and raised it quickly, trying to throw the snake, but it landed behind him near Frank and Lyle. Both jumped, but Frank took his stick and successfully threw it to the dry dirt up away from the creek.

We all got out to look at it and could hear a type of rattling. Ronnie said, "Stay back. That's a poisonous timber rattler. See the big rattle at the end of its tail. I want that rattle to show to my scout troop so help me kill the snake." We gathered big rocks and smashed the snake to smithereens. Ronnie caught off the tail and put it in his little "be prepared" scout bag. We loved the three-mile creek, and that was the only dangerous snake we ever saw there. But the bloodsuckers continued to like us.

BY THE SCRUFF OF MY NECK

Another place we played in the water was in a creek behind a nursing home, only two miles away. There was a small decorative dam to make a gentle waterfall. We went skinny dipping there once in a while but usually got chased out. We also swam in gorgeous Lake Ontario both at the wonderful Camp Hollis and also regular beaches all along the lakeshore.

The main relevance to all of this is that we were all very experienced in all types of water from six years old and on up. Now Peter came into the home at seven years old and never swam and was deathly afraid of water. His first lesson was in a closed-in swimming pool where the shallow end was up to his neck and the teacher kept stressing loudly for him to relax. By simple observation, I learned then and there that intimidation will never work.

After class, I talked to Peter and told him about our trips to the lake, and he can come with us. I put my arm around his shoulder and told him, "I don't care if you don't learn to swim. Just stay close to the shore in your bathing suit so I can keep my eye on you." Then I started some fun games in the shallow water with the other boys, mainly just having fun tossing beach balls, volleyballs, and whatever around—lots of splashing, diving in to get something, and always laughter, for no reason, just laughing.

Several times, I would accidentally on purpose bat the ball to Peter. He would pick it up and throw it back in. After a few times, he stayed standing at the edge of the water and was included in the games. Soon he was in up to his calves and before long over his knees. He slipped a couple of times and fell right into the water. The dunking didn't deter him; he got up laughing to my amazement!

Now that I knew he could get completely wet without any trauma, I suggested a new game. I said, "Let's play fishing pole bobber. Everyone tucks their chin to their chest and brings their knees up to their chins and wraps their arms around them. You will sink to the bottom but then come bobbing back to the surface. A very fun experience." We all did it many times, including Peter.

A day or two later, I reminded him of the bobber game, and he said it was fun. I said, "The next game is even more fun. We start the same way but instead of bobbing we thrust our hands out forward and stretched our feet to float straight back. If you just float, that is called 'the dead man's float.' If you can thrust or surface dive, then you become a powerful torpedo.'" He did both of these quickly on one quiet morning. Over the next few days, we gave the torpedo some swinging arms and kicking feet. In just a few more days, Peter was swimming!

I was so proud of him, and he began joining us on all of our weird adventures. He was never called chicken again. And for the first time, I knew I wanted to become a teacher.

CHAPTER 14

The Tracks and the Pier

As I woke up one hot, humid Saturday in July, I wondered what I would do today. "Floyd, what do you want to do today?"

He answered, "Anything, what about you?"

"I don't know either, but let's think of something before everybody else does."

After a little more thought, I said, "I would like to finish that hike we started, you know, the one on the railroad tracks. I never found out for sure where the tracks went, but it was easy to tell that they headed north toward the lake."

Floyd said, "Nah, it's way too hot and humid to take that hike."

I kept thinking about it. My head had a mind of its own sometimes, and it became preoccupied with following those tracks. Finally, a lightbulb flashed in my head. "If we got an early start, it wouldn't be too hot yet. And as it got hotter and if the tracks went to the lake, then we could cool off in the water before noon."

Floyd went, "Hey, Craig, that's a big if, but it sounds like it could work. But you tell the other guys."

I said, "I'll just ask them if they want to join us." Five of our usual seven guys agreed: Ronnie the scout, Lyle the lion, Johnny the daredevil, and Floyd and I.

I was surprised that Frank and Bobby Potter didn't want to go. I asked Frank if he had something else better to do. He replied, "Nope, just don't feel like going today." I was so excited I finished my breakfast and chores in double time. Now I was standing out by the lane between the garden and root cellar with the playground behind me waiting for the others to hurry up.

Craig at eleven years old waiting for his fellow hikers to join him.

Once our chores and breakfasts were done, I started walking toward the marsh south of the pasture. The other four joined in. It seemed a lot shorter walking this time, especially with the marshy area drying up along with Curly's pond. Soon the train tracks were in sight. I hollered, "Yea, we made it." No train cars today, so I just stepped up on a track and started my tight rope act just walking north on the track.

Floyd said, "Let's see who can go the farthest without falling off."

One of Ronnie's feet touched the ground. Lyle said, "Ronnie you are out."

Ronnie responded, "No way, I didn't fall off. My foot just dropped a little like a real tight rope walker. I saw it in the movies."

Lyle said, "You are a cheater. Admit it."

I was starting to get nervous as a big fight would ruin our hike. "Let's think of something else to do while we are walking," I said.

Johnny said, "Walk backward on the track." But no one could do it.

My heart jumped as we got closer to Lake Ontario. The tracks went right up to a very large building with four giant smokestacks. "Wow," I exclaimed. "What is that?"

Ronnie said, "It's a steam plant for generating power and even electricity. I'll bet it burns a lot of coal! See how the railroad tracks go right up to that equipment on the side of the plant."

I thought that it would be fun to watch the coal being lifted out of the train cars by that equipment and moved into the plant and made a note in the back of my head. "I can't wait to get back and tell Frank and Bobby what they missed," I said.

Floyd said, "Yeah, they are going to be sorry."

Johnny said, "Let's walk around to the other side."

The huge steam plant had a fence around it that was twice as wide as the plant itself. So it took a few minutes to walk around it. The fence took us right up to the lake which had a harbor where ships could come in and get coal and other cargo. We saw a long pier made out of boulders and concrete. Ronnie said it was a breakwater, not a pier. It went due north for a quarter mile and then turned northeast and went another half mile before it turned north again. I could see a lighthouse at the northern tip which was another half mile. The Oswego River fed into the lake at this point with another breakwater on the east side going straight north. The two breakwaters enclosed a nice quiet calm water harbor with a small entrance at the northernmost tips. On the lakeside of the breakwaters, there were a lot of waves washing right up and over the boulders.

Who could resist this adventure? We all started walking out on the breakwater, and I was determined to reach the lighthouse. The first part of the trip was quite easy with no dangers.

The beginning of the breakwater was very smooth and easy to walk. Photo by Craig Fisher.

Very smooth concrete, but things changed at the last turn to the north, no smooth concrete surfaces—just enormous boulders dumped every which way. There were lots of openings where I could see water down below. It was tough going—half climbing up and down and half walking. Johnny wanted to play tag. I said, "No way, not me."

Johnny called, "What are you a chicken?" I ignored him, and so did the others.

Nobody got hurt, but there were a few banged-up knees. And we all got splashed a lot. I said, "See, we got cooled off by the lake."

The rough part of the breakwater. Picture from DOD web page.

BY THE SCRUFF OF MY NECK

The continuation of the breakwater to the lighthouse. DOD web page.

My goal was reached, but a little disappointing as there was nothing new at the lighthouse. It was locked uptight. Ronnie, looking due north, wondered out loud to no one in particular, "How far is Canada from here?"

No one knew for sure, but Floyd said, "Hey, I can see the trees across the lake, so it can't be too far."

Lyle said, "Maybe we could get a rowboat and cross over. It would be a perfect way to run away and the home people would never find us."

Johnny said, "Yeah, let's do it." Running away from everything was always on our minds.

"Just think how peaceful life would be over there. No more rubber slippers," Floyd said. I agreed as I looked over the smooth and peaceful lake. I thought that this was one dream that we all shared.

But then Ronnie said, "I don't think so. Let me get some maps and find out how far it would be to get to Canada. And Floyd, those aren't trees, just shadows."

Turning around, we could see the steam plant, the river, the college, lots of buildings, and houses. We scrambled back to the beginning of the breakwater. I figured we covered about three miles to get to the steam plant and another mile and a quarter to get to the lighthouse. So altogether, the hike today took us about nine miles. I said, "Let's jump in the lake before we start back." No arm twisting there. I saw some other kids swimming between the steam plant and the college. I suggested we go where they are as it must have a better beach than most of the lake, which has mostly rocky beaches.

After about a half hour of swimming, we decided to head home. We all dreaded the walk home. Johnny noticed that the other kids pretty far from the shore left their bicycles up on the high ground and said, "Let's ride home. Those rich city kids can buy new ones any time they want."

Ronnie said, "What if we get caught?"

Lyle laughed and said, "Who's going to catch us? Come on, before they see us."

Johnny said, "Yeah, and we can dump them before we get back to the home."

I wish I could say I resisted, but I went along with the plan. We now moved from stealing church donations, small amounts from stores and milk trucks, to stealing major things that cost a lot of money. I wondered how bad those other kids are going to feel when they find their bikes missing. We dumped the bikes in an empty field with deep grass several blocks from the home. Nothing else was ever mentioned about it. I felt guilty. A feeling of doom and gloom washed over me.

When we got home, I was dying to tell Frank what he missed: the railroad tracks, the steam plant, the breakwater, the lighthouse, and a good swim. He and Bobby were not around. We were just in time for dinner. Frank and Bobby were not at dinner either. At bedtime, still no sign of Frank and Bobby. Floyd said, "Don't worry. He is a big guy who can take care of himself. He'll probably get back late tonight."

I said, "I am not worried, just wondering." The next morning found no sign of Frank or Bobby.

CHAPTER 15

Mystery Solved

The next day after breakfast, Mrs. Wyatt, the headmistress of the boys, called me over. She seemed very concerned and asked me, "Where is Frank?"

I answered, "I don't know."

She pressured me, "Craig, you must know. He wouldn't just disappear without telling you what he was up to."

I said, "I don't know. I and some of the other guys went on a hike, and Frank didn't want to go. That was the last I saw of him. When we got back from the hike, I looked for him but couldn't find him."

She said, "Well, we are all worried about him. Maybe he had an accident somewhere. Mrs. Dick, headmistress of the entire children's home, will want to talk to you. She is calling the police, and they want to meet with you. So you better be ready to tell us everything."

I said, "I told you all I know, which is nothing."

About an hour later, I talked with Richard Potter, Bobby's brother. He said, "Yeah, Mrs. Wyatt asked me the same things and warned me that Mrs. Dick is really mad."

I said, "I hate being called up in front of Mrs. Dick as she is liable to punish us no matter how innocent we are. I wonder if she is afraid of losing her job if something happened to some of the boys. The caretakers, Mrs. Wyatt, and Mrs. Dick had no clue where we were all day. Of course, I could never tell her exactly where we hiked and everything we did." I started sweating bullets. "Richard, do you know where Frank and Bobby are?"

He said, "Nope, but we are probably in for it."

Another hour or so went by, and then Mrs. Reese came to our playroom and said, "Craig, Mrs. Dick wants to meet with you now."

So I followed Mrs. Reese down to Mrs. Dick's office. She was not alone. Her assistant director, Mrs. Reese, stayed with us, and a cop stood there. They spent half their time telling me how serious it was for Frank and Bobby to disappear like that. Mrs. Dick said, "I know how close you and Frank are, and he would never leave voluntarily without telling you. So where is he?"

I blurted out, "I just don't know."

Then the cop jumped in with "Son, you have to tell us since Frank could be in danger. Maybe he got hurt, or worse, maybe he got kidnapped. You wouldn't want anything to happen to him, or would you?"

I thought, *If anyone tried to kidnap Frank and Bobby, then the kidnappers would be in for a lot of trouble that they didn't bargain for.* "I just don't know!" I stammered.

The cop followed with "If he did run away, where do you think he might go? Did he ever talk about running away?"

I thought, *Of course, everybody did. It's just these kinds of talks that make one want to get the hell out of here.*

"Where would Frank most likely go? Any clue you can give us might save Frank a world of problems." After a long quiet pause, the dirty copper continued, "Come on, son, give us something to go on."

I am sweating now and on the verge of tears. I could feel both the water welling up in my eyes and sweat dripping down my forehead. I repeated, "I just don't know."

Mrs. Dick said, "You don't have to play tonight after supper. You can just go to bed and think about it. Tonight I am calling your father to come here tomorrow to try and talk some sense into you."

After supper, I met Richard on the way up to bed. He got the same treatment that I did. He knew exactly what I knew, nothing. Richard said, "The good news is that neither of us got the rubber slipper."

BY THE SCRUFF OF MY NECK

I said, "I would rather get the rubber slipper and get it over with. Now I am going to have a long talk and get another lecture from Pop."

Sure enough, Pop arrived at the children's home midmorning the next day—the beginning of the third day with no sign of or word from Frank or Bobby. He went directly to Mrs. Dick's office and talked to her privately for quite a while. Meanwhile, I sat in the visitor's room waiting for Pop. After about half an hour, Pop walked into the visitors' room. He took very slow short steps, and he bent his head downward. His eyes bulged out, and he looked left and right a few times. This gave me sympathy for him and what he must be going through. He never misses even an hour of work as a leather cutter in a pocketbook factory in downtown Syracuse. This was very stressful for him, but the conversation went nowhere.

His questions seemed more thoughtful and more caring than the cops and Mrs. Dick's. Pop asked me, "What friends in the community might take Frank in for a while?"

I said, "Frank has a lot of friends all around, but I have no guesses as to who would take him in."

He then asked, "Have any kids left the home over the past year or so and moved to their own home somewhere in the area?"

I said, "Kids come and go all the time, but I can't keep track of them and have no idea where to look."

I was a lot more comfortable talking like this with Pop. He was more relaxed and genuinely interested in Frank's welfare. Also, he didn't challenge everything I said. He trusted me, and I trusted him. Besides I have no memory of him ever punishing me.

I told Pop, "One friend, Jimmy Condon, got out last year and moved to a village called Mexico just a few miles from here."

So Pop went and got permission for him to take me on a drive with him up to Mexico. Of course, it was quickly granted. Mrs. Reese also gave Condon's address to Pop. He wanted to drive up instead of making a phone call. He said face-to-face is better because he can see their facial expressions and body language and know if they are hiding anything. We found their house with no problem, but the meeting was next to useless. Jimmy had no idea of Frank's whereabouts but said, "The next time we see Frank, give my congratulations to Frank for getting away."

Pop stared at Jimmy for a minute and then said, "Thank you," and we left.

Back in the village of Oswego, we drove along the lake and then up and down along the river. We also went to that creek area behind the nursing home. We even walked on the railroad tracks to the linemen's shack, but there was no sign of Frank or Bobby anywhere. After, Pop bought me a couple of hotdogs for a late lunch at Rudy's hotdog stand on Lake Ontario. Then he dropped me back at the home, met with Mrs. Dick for a few minutes, and left.

The fourth day came and went. The fifth and sixth days had the same results, i.e., nothing. All of the kids could not stop talking about the situation. They were cheering Frank and Bobby saying, "They have been away longer than anybody in the history of the home." There was much speculation guessing where they might be.

Lyle said, "They probably got a boat and crossed Lake Ontario to Canada."

Ronnie said, "Not likely. I looked up the width of Lake Ontario on my scout map, and it is twenty-six miles wide. There are also a lot of ships crisscrossing the lake. If they tried that, then they probably drowned."

I said, "Oh no, don't say that. I hope not."

On the afternoon of the seventh day, a patrol car pulled up to the home with two boys in it—Frank and Bobby. They stayed in the office for a long time, but I couldn't leave the area as I was dying to find out what happened.

Once out of the office, I and the others crowded around Frank and Bobby. I said, "Boy, am I glad to see you, guys! Pop even came up during the week to look for you. I and Pop were really worried about you. What happened?"

Frank said, "Nothing much, just a long hike."

I badgered him a little and said, "Seven days is not some small hike."

"Well," he replied, "we were told not to talk about it, but here goes a short version. Bobby and I ran away. We stored some food up

BY THE SCRUFF OF MY NECK

for the last week or so and even took a change of clothes. We hitch-hiked west and got rides here and there."

"Wow," I exclaimed. "How far did you get? You were gone a week!"

"We made it to Rochester, which is around seventy-five miles."

Floyd said, "That's a world record. No one ever stayed out that long and got that far."

Frank started to smile at that and said, "We slept in a couple of barns and the fields a couple of nights. We ate a lot of apples and vegetables that we were able to pick in some farms." As the talk continued, I could tell that they were both proud of their accomplishment.

I said, "Hey, Frank, I wish you told me your plans. I was quite worried, especially after Pop came up. Don't you trust me?"

He simply said, "I know you are not a squealer, but Pop might wear you down trying to scare you by saying that something might happen to me. So you would have to help Pop find me. That's why I dropped hints over the previous week about wishing to see Jimmy Condon in Mexico again someday. You did try to help Pop, right?"

I responded, "Yeah, I did. But the disappearance with no word was a real mystery, and I got scared for you." That ended the conversation, but I thought if we had talked about it and I knew his plans, then I would not give him up.

Finally, I asked, "How did you get caught?"

Frank said, "We ran into a real heavy thunderstorm and got so soaked we were freezing, also got a little hungry. So we stopped at a farmhouse and told them we were on an overnight hike, but the rainstorm ruined our tent. Maybe you would let us dry off and stay overnight—just one night." Both husband and wife were there and readily agreed. They even fed us a very nice hot dinner. While the wife was doing that, the husband was gone for a few minutes. The next morning, he said, "I am taking you guys for a ride."

Bobby continued, "Of all the bad luck, he was a state trooper and had read about us in various police reports. He drove us back to Oswego and turned us over to the local police."

Frank said, "That about sums it up."

CHAPTER 16

The Turning Point

Someone got greedy and blew it for all of us. We knew it wouldn't last forever, but our gravy train ran out the day Ronnie took the whole box. What a shocker that our trusted scout was the culprit. I guessed he needed the money for some scout supplies, but I never knew for sure. We were all guilty of taking some change and putting it in our pockets. We pooled our money so it would add up after a while so we could buy baseballs and new mitts—instead of stealing them.

It was easy pickings. The milk truck delivered large farm-size cans of milk every few days at around 10:00 a.m. during the summer. The delivery point was inside the U behind the main building and sided by the girls' dorm on one side and the boys' dorm on the other side. It was easy to access because the milkman parked and took the milk into the kitchen. Bobby Potter noticed that the milkman left the truck quite open when he took a can inside the building. Peeking inside the truck, Bobby saw a cigar box full of change. He started cleverly by taking only a few coins that would never be missed.

After a while, we all took our share. This continued for weeks until Ronnie took the whole box for himself. "Are you nuts, Ronnie?" I screamed.

"Now the milkman can't miss seeing our dirty work!"

Floyd chimed in, "And he will know exactly where he was when the box disappeared!"

Ronnie said, "Just keep quiet, and he can't prove anything."

BY THE SCRUFF OF MY NECK

The milkman was clever too, and he was already on to us. When he took the cans of milk inside, he would look out the window to watch the activity around the truck. He spotted us and kept a record in a notebook for a few weeks. Then when the whole box disappeared, he reported us to Mrs. Dick, headmistress of the home. She demanded punishment for us all but didn't call the police. She just told Stafford to take care of it.

Stafford gave the rubber slipper to everyone he heard had been involved except he didn't catch Norm yet. Norm Wallace was a tiger and the only one who ever gave my brother Frank a tie fight by mutual fatigue. Whenever they fought, blood spattered everywhere until they both were too tired to punch anymore. Otherwise, they remained friends.

Finally, Stafford caught up to Norm in the gymnasium where we had been learning to fight. Stafford grabbed Norm by the arm and started swatting him with a rubber slipper. Norm fought to get loose. Norm's brother Fred saw this going on, so he jumped on Stafford's back. But the two Wallace boys alone weren't quite enough to subdue Stafford. Two more boys heard the ruckus and rushed over to help gang up on Stafford. The four toughened teenage boys not only subdued Stafford but beat him for every punishment he ever dealt out over the past couple of years. Stafford got his due that day.

The four boys went to jail for a week, but one never came back. Carl went on to a reform school while the other three came back home. We never saw caretaker Stafford again and have no idea what went down with him.

The replacement caretaker marked a turning point for all of us. While we were all wondering who would take over as caretaker, we were introduced to the tallest person that I ever saw, a giant. He introduced himself as Mr. Johanessen but immediately smiled and said, "Call me Mr. John." He was six foot five. He began by asking our names and what kinds of things that we like to do. The replies were pretty consistent. "I like sports and hiking and swimming" was blurted out by more than half the kids. Hiking took the limelight given our recent experiences on the railroad tracks, coal cars, and the breakwaters.

"Where do you like to hike?" he asked. "Are there good places nearby?"

Frank said, "Sure, just south of our pasture, there are some trails that lead to some railroad tracks where we have seen train cars." We then all walked around the edge of the property, and he listened to everything we had to say about any of our activities. He laughed hard when we told him about trying to catch a skunk and laughed harder when I told him Curly bit me when we tried to ride him. He promised to go with us on a hike this coming Saturday. He said due to prior commitments and that he needed to speak more about other things with both Mrs. Dick and Mrs. Wyatt, he said that he was quite sure we could go Saturday.

That night it was hard to get to sleep. Floyd whispered to me from the next bed, "What do you think of Mr. John?"

I whispered back, "I don't know, he seemed nice."

Lyle jumped in with "Let's see if he goes hiking with us on Saturday."

Frank said, "Yeah, hard to trust any of these caretakers."

I liked Mr. John's smile and told everyone. Floyd said, "That's the first time any of them ever walked around our playground with us. He seemed interested in where we played."

Frank agreed, "True, true, but wait and see."

I said, "Yeah, our fathers never even came out here to see any of it."

Ronnie made another good point, "Remember when Mr. John asked about the big fence between the two playgrounds and we said, 'It's because boys and girls weren't allowed to play with each other?' Mr. John simply said 'hmmm,' but let it drop. I wondered why he did that."

Frank finally said, "Go to sleep and we'll find out on Saturday if he is just another rubber slipper guy." With that, I drifted off to sleep.

Although Mr. John's arrival was a turning point that replaced rubber slippers with kindness, interest, and friendliness, it did not mean that we were quite finished with getting into trouble.

CHAPTER 17

A New Counselor

The week dragged on. I was so excited when Mr. John came back on Saturday. He gathered a bunch of us together around 9:00 a.m. and said, "Let's go on that hike."

I shouted, "Yea, I knew he would do it!"

He replied, "Just show me the way," our usual seven boys, plus Mr. John.

I asked, "How about letting Billy and Roy join us this time?"

Mr. John said, "Sure," and off we went. We knew the way well from so many hikes down to the tracks that we made it in record time. I couldn't see any train cars, so I said, "Mr. John, I hope you are not disappointed that there were no coal cars."

He replied, "Not at all, maybe next time!"

Lyle said, "There's the railroad detectives' shack where two men came out and tried to chase us."

Mr. John said, "I'll bet you guys could outrun them any day of the week."

I thought, *Boy, this guy is cool. He seemed to like the idea that we were adventurous.* He even said, "You guys could build one like it."

"Wow, what a great idea. We could make a clubhouse," I said.

Floyd said, "Where, here?"

Frank said, "We can't do it here. But there is a nice flat area up where you jerks tried to ride Curly." The sound of a train coming

75

down the tracks made us drop that subject abruptly, but the seed was planted.

The train, with its dozen or more full coal cars and coming into the city, was moving pretty slowly. Mr. John asked, "Have any of you ever tried to ride one of the trains?" I was shocked at such a question from a caretaker. He told us, "When it's moving so slowly, you can run alongside it at the same speed until the ladder handles will almost look they are standing still so you can just reach up and grab on. But once you grab on, you have got to hold on tight as your feet will immediately leave the ground."

All of us, but Billy and Roy did it with no problem. I thought this was one of our most exciting hikes ever. I said, "This big train ride was better than any carnival ride I ever went on." Everyone agreed. We spent a lot of time that summer between the harbor's water-breaks and the trains in addition to our usual game playing on the catwalks under the bridges.

Mr. John also took us on other adventures. He drove us in the home's GMC truck to the college beaches along Lake Ontario, as well as to historical Fort Ontario on the east side of the harbor. The college was only two miles from the home, and the fort was three miles. Our summers were full of adventures. When he took us to the fort, he arranged free passes for us to get in; but when we went alone, we were supposed to pay to get in. Not liking that we walked around to the far side of the fort and climbed up the stone walls and were able to get in. I was impressed with all the cannons, guns, exhibits; and we also played lots of games. After a while, the guards noticed us and chased us out of there hollering, "Never come back." This made us all laugh—of course, we'd come back.

BY THE SCRUFF OF MY NECK

Side view of Fort Ontario. Photograph by Craig Fisher

One day, on the way home from the fort, we walked up the road past our favorite bridges and went south along the river. At one point, not too far from the home, there was an interesting area of the river. It had a dam and waterfall about halfway across the river. I asked, "Why would they ever build only half a dam?"

Frank explained, "The other half was a section where boats could go through, and those were locks that raised or lowered the water so boats could get to the lake without touching the bottom."

I said, "I wish we could go swimming down there at the bottom of the falls. I see a lot of big, flat rocks we could play on."

Frank replied, "I don't see why not. All we have to do is climb over this fence and some paths lead to the bottom."

Lyle said, "What are we waiting for?" And down we went. I felt a little guilty about the sign that said "no admittance." Everyone had fun, and we got home just in the nick of time for dinner. I slept like a log that night.

DR. CRAIG W. FISHER

A partial dam across half of the Oswego River made an ideal place for swimming and adventures. Photo by Craig Fisher.

I think the presence of Mr. John was a major turning point in most of our lives. He immersed himself in our lives. Nobody ever saw a rubber slipper again. I think I started to learn a lifelong lesson that summer that kindness and interest are far more effective than physical discipline. But nothing is perfect.

The next morning, Frank said, "Does anyone want to build a clubhouse like the one we talked about with Mr. John?"

I said, "Yeah," and the others were also very excited about it.

Ronnie said, "We'll need to get wood, hammers, and nails." I said, "Where and how? We can't afford to buy them." But I couldn't guess how we did it so successfully.

CHAPTER 18

The Clubhouse

I saved up and then spent every extra nickel or dime that I could scrape up, even off the floor at the Knights of Columbus at Christmastime, on buying plastic models. So far, I bought and built six models—two aircraft carriers, a battleship, a destroyer, and two airplanes. But now they were getting in everybody's way. Raymond smashed one with a ball. I screamed at him, "Why did you do that?"

He yelled back, "It was an accident, okay!"

I said, "Yeah, but can't you be more careful?"

He replied, "Who do you think you are, a big shot? You can't be setting your models all around the playroom. Other people live here too you know."

Mrs. Wyatt heard the ruckus and scurried over and said, "Raymond's right, a lot of kids play in this room."

"So what am I supposed to do anyhow?" I shot back.

She said, "You can't leave your models on the big table in the middle of the playroom. You'll have to figure something else out."

I went to bed thinking about it and came up with an idea. The next morning, I said, "Mrs. Wyatt I think that the space between that big TV cabinet and the corner of the wall would be pretty safe. If I make a small table and put it there and set my models on it, would that be okay with you?"

She said, "Yes, but still no guarantees."

DR. CRAIG W. FISHER

Well, building a table was harder than I thought. I believed it would be simple. First, I needed to find some boards, a saw, a hammer, and some nails. I started exploring the best place—the barn. I got some nails and a hammer in the barn but did not find a saw or any boards. I told Floyd my dilemma, and he suggested that I search the basement. I knew it was against the rules, but I snuck down one evening. I found a saw in a storeroom. Now all I needed were some boards. I just kept scouring the area, including the barn again, the root cellar, and other rooms in the basement. Finally, I found a bunch of mismatched old boards behind the barn. Little did I know that they were thrown away for a reason. The boards seemed a little soft, but I was determined to go ahead.

I cut and made four three-foot-long boards. I laid them snugly together on the ground. Then I nailed three pieces of wood across the bottom. This took a little doing since some of my nails couldn't stick in the softwood. But soon I had my tabletop. Now all I had to do was to make four boards about three feet long and nail them at the corners for legs. Again, this took longer than planned as the softwood was not very strong. Finally, I got it done, and it didn't bother me one iota that the legs were not like posts but just boards nailed into the edges of the tabletop. It didn't bother me either that a couple of legs were nailed in along the side and a couple at the ends. It didn't matter to me at all that I didn't paint it nor refinish it in any way.

Floyd saw my job and said, "Craig, I hate to tell you, but that looks like junk. And it doesn't look very strong."

I said, "It doesn't have to be strong. It's just going to sit in a corner protected by that big TV cabinet and hold my very light plastic models. And it won't matter how it looks since my models will cover it."

I was very happy to bring it in when no one was around. I set it in the corner as planned and put my five remaining models on it. Later, Mrs. Wyatt saw it and hollered, "Get that piece of rotten wood out of here right now. It looks like hell. That rotten wood is probably full of insects that will soon be crawling all over the building." She busted my balloon. In a combination of shame and anger, I took it outside, leaving my models on the floor in the corner. When I came in, Mrs. Wyatt said, "I'm sorry Craig. I shouldn't have hollered at you like that, but I did get worried about bugs infiltrating the place."

She followed with "I have been thinking about your dilemma and have a solution for you. In the older boys' library, there are a set of bookshelves that have glass doors, and there is some room there. You can keep your models there."

"Wow, really?" I exclaimed.

She said, "Yes, but you can't just go in there whenever you want. You'll need permission."

I thought, *Yeah I know that. I'm only nine years old and that room is for teenagers.* Frank was only 10.5, but he could go in there because he was bigger than most of them anyhow.

But I replied, "Yea! Anything you say. You just made me very happy. Thank you." After I put the models in the book cabinet and came back out, I looked over at Mrs. Wyatt sitting in her big chair. She was smiling. While I still had only a modest collection of models, this step gave me the encouragement to increase the collection as it gave me a safe place to put the models.

Pictured here are over twenty models in my collection at the time the home closed. I snapped this picture shortly after moving into my mother's apartment in Syracuse when the children's home closed. In less than a year, she dumped them because they took up too much space in her apartment.

DR. CRAIG W. FISHER

A few days later, I noticed Frank, Lyle, and his brother Dewitt, Ronnie, and his brother Clinton all sitting around a table in the library. I told Floyd, and he said, "They must be having a meeting."

I said, "Thanks for nothing. I could guess that much. But what about?"

Floyd responded, "Who knows?"

I said, "I'm going in and find out."

He told me, "Don't do it. You'll get in trouble, and they probably won't tell you anyway."

"Okay, let's see," I said as I opened the doors and walked in.

Dewitt said, "Hey, Craig, you can't be in here. You better leave."

I said, "I can as I have permission to look in and check on my models."

Frank said, "Let him stay. He's not hurting anybody." Nobody argued with Frank.

I overheard them talking about building a clubhouse as Mr. John suggested back when we were down by the railroad tracks a few weeks ago. I said, "Hey, count me and Floyd in. We can build and help a lot."

Dewitt said, "I don't think so. We saw that table you built, and we still can't stop laughing."

Frank said, "Lighten up. We can use them for gofers."

"What does an animal like a gopher have to do with it?" I questioned. They all laughed a little bit.

Then Frank said, "It means that you go for this, or you go for that. You run errands for us to save time."

I said, "Okay, we can do that."

When I told Floyd, he said, "I told you that table looked like junk."

I said, "All right, already. Let's just do what we can to help so they don't lock us out of it."

That night, Frank said, "After supper, we are going to search for some good boards."

He looked at me and said, "No rotten boards." Everyone laughed. Lyle and Bobby said they saw a huge stack of boards behind someone's house not far from the woodsy corner of the pasture.

BY THE SCRUFF OF MY NECK

Lyle said, "All we have to do is wait until dark and then sneak from that back corner along the property fences until we come to the pile of boards."

Bobby said, "It's perfect. At night, no one will ever see us going along the hedges and fences."

Six of us met down in the woodsy patch around 8:00 p.m. Frank said, "Okay, we are going to spread out in a long single line. Then we'll be able to simply pass the boards along the line. You'll have to take the board when it is passed to you and carry it a few yards and give it to the next guy and then come back. Any questions?" Frank was first and passed to Lyle who passed to Bobby and then Bobby to me. I passed to Floyd who passed to Johnny who passed to Ronnie. Ronnie stacked the boards so that they were well hidden in the woods. It was going great for about the first seven boards. Then we heard some dogs barking. Moments later, some lights went on and flashed all around us. We all took off running like crazy. A very heavy loud voice shouted, "What are you doing there? Got off my property, or I'll send the dogs after you."

We just kept running, and this time, no one was laughing. I said, "I hope he doesn't call the police."

Lyle said, "Probably not as he has so many boards he wouldn't even be able to tell if anything was missing."

We left the boards in the woods for several days. Then one day, Mr. John asked, "Aren't you guys ever going to build a shack?" Frank told Mr. John the truth about what happened. Mr. John earned our trust, and we never lied to him. Mr. John pondered the problem for several minutes and finally said, "Stealing is not a good idea, but if you must, don't get caught. If the lights go on, just lay down in the grass. Don't move a muscle. Soon the owner will go back into his house. Then take the boards you already started with and walk slowly back to the pasture."

Frank said, "Okay, we can do that."

Mr. John followed with "I still don't advise stealing. And never go back to the same house twice."

Over the next three weeks, we accumulated enough boards to start building. The older guys did all the main work while Floyd,

Johnny, and I ran for more nails as needed. Then our job got harder. They told us to find some chairs or stools or anything we could sit on inside the clubhouse when it's finished. Bobby said, "Let's go check out the lineman's shack and see if they have anything we can use." We found a nice wooden rocking chair and brought it back, and it fit nicely in the clubhouse.

Lyle said, "Good start. Now go find something else. Go downtown to the dump and see what you can find."

We did and came back with an old badly worn car seat. It took four of us to carry it. Frank said, "Hey great! That will make a perfect couch." Running out of ideas, we just got a couple of old wooden crates from the basement and stood them on end to use as stools.

We spent many hours in the clubhouse during the rest of the summer. We told the same old jokes over and over. We talked about forming a real baseball team and entering it into the city recreation league. We talked about how nice Mr. John was. And we did a lot of teasing each other. Ronnie said, "Hey, Craig, when are you going to make your next table?" We all laughed, even me. I taught myself two things. One was that if they tease you, they like you. At least I always hoped that was the case. And two, if you get defensive, they will just do it more and more. Over the years, I learned that the hard way.

Mr. John came down to the clubhouse several times. He complimented the whole team saying, "Nice job. You all were very creative. I liked seeing all you guys working together. Where did you get the couch and rocking chair?"

This time, I lied. I said, "We found them at the dump." I thought, *By that look on his face, I know he doesn't believe that chair came from the dump.* But he didn't say any more about it. I just looked down at my feet.

After a couple of months, the unbelievable happened. In the middle of the night, Floyd woke me up and stammered, "Look outside." I noticed everybody was up and lining up by the back windows looking toward a big glow at the edge of the pasture. I heard sirens blaring and saw lots of red lights flashing. I asked, "What's going on?"

Frank replied, "The clubhouse is burning down."

BY THE SCRUFF OF MY NECK

I said, "Holy smoke. That can't be?"

Ronnie said, "Maybe one of you guys was smoking in there and weren't careful about putting out your cigarettes?"

Weeks went by before we found out what might have happened. We went back to our routine, hike down on the railroad tracks. We looked into the lineman's shack and saw the rocking chair.

CHAPTER 19

Baseball

CAMP HOLLIS

One of the best things about living in the children's home was when we went to Camp Hollis for two weeks every summer. This was like going to heaven after living in the home all year. Most of the counselors were young enthusiastic men and women from Oswego State Teachers College. Around seven thirty every morning, Keith or Jake came into our dorm room that held all twenty of the boys and hollered, "What are you still doing in bed? It is time to get up and get going. We have a lot to do today!" After washing and getting dressed, he led us into the dining area where we could sit wherever we wanted, even among some of the girls. Yes, believe it or not, boys and girls actually ate and played together! The tables were covered with little boxes of cereal, large pitchers of milk, and fruit juice.

I asked Keith, "What things can I eat?"

Keith said, "What? Eat anything you want and as much as you want." Lunches were almost the same.

When we filed in for lunch, Keith always boomed out, "What's your favorite sandwich?"

Our chorus response was "peanut butter and jelly!"

Keith shouted back, "What? I can't hear you." So louder and louder it went.

BY THE SCRUFF OF MY NECK

Once he found out the type of sandwiches we liked, he boomed out, "What's your favorite jelly?"

We all yelled, "Smucker's."

"C'mon, you, guys, say it so I can hear you!"

Soon I was screaming my head off, "Smucker's." Most of the dinners were like going on big picnics. They cooked hotdogs, hamburgers, cheeseburgers, and served macaroni and potato salads, watermelons, and the like. As dusk approached, Keith asked, "What are you waiting for? Go collect some firewood so we can have a bonfire." We ate marshmallows and sang typical camp songs. I went to bed so happy every night.

Your two weeks were determined by age, and most of the home kids were from a year and a half to three years older than me. So only Johnny and I went together every year. In addition to all the usual camp activities like hiking, swimming in Lake Ontario in the mornings and afternoons, the counselors formed us into a baseball team. We played real games against guest teams bussed in from other parks, recreation leagues, and little league teams. We practiced or played every day, but no one else wanted to be a catcher. All the other boys refused to get behind the plate. I said, "I'd like to give it a try." I knew that by doing so, I would always have a spot on the team and that I would play the whole game. Now all I had to do was learn how to catch. It wasn't as easy as I expected. I wasn't afraid of the batter hitting me with the bat, but there was a lot to learn.

Counselor Keith was a catcher himself and worked with me every day. Soon I could handle low or high pitches easily. I could throw runners out, trying to steal second base. I learned to hold the glove in the strike zone for many seconds after a pitch to give the umpire some assistance to realize that the pitch was a strike and not a ball. I encouraged the pitcher by saying things like, "You're doing great. You got this guy," or the usual, "Hum, babe, put it in there." And I hollered at the batters, "You're an easy out. You swing like an old lady. Where'd you learn to bat anyhow, at the zoo in a monkey cage?"

At the home, I had to play with much older kids most of the time, and that helped me a lot in the Camp Hollis games. When playing in my age group, I was our best hitter—batting third or fourth in every game—and I was our only catcher. We won most of our games, and my name was in Oswego's *The Palladium-Times* a few times. At the end of our second week, the counselors lined us up and led us onto the bus checking off our names. Surprising and embarrassing myself, I cried as the bus headed to the home. Other kids got dropped off at regular bus stops and were greeted by their parents. Johnny and I were the last two boys to get off.

Baseball Team

Back at the home, we played a lot of flies and grounders" but usually couldn't get enough guys together to play a regular game amongst ourselves. That would take at least eighteen boys all at the same time and for a couple of hours. Floyd, Frank, and I were analyzing the problem. I asked, "What do you guys think we can do about it?"

Floyd suggested, "Maybe we can get some city kids to come and play against us."

Frank said, "Good idea. I'll ask some of my friends to round up a bunch to come and play some games. But now we have to get organized. I can pitch." Floyd claimed second base or shortstop. Frank went on, "Okay, let's tell the other guys." Our regulars were all in on it, and we had a couple of newer guys who would play. Ronnie took shortstop, Jim Condon third base, Jim Galloway took first base. Lyle, Johnny, and Bobby took outfield.

I chimed in, "A counselor at Camp Hollis taught me to be a catcher so I want to be the catcher." In a pinch, Dewitt said he could play first base, and Clinton said he could help anywhere also.

Dewitt said, "But I'm not coming to practices. I can already play."

Clinton added, "Me too, I have enough to do. Just let me know when the games are and if you need me to play."

The pipsqueaks, Roy and Billy, said, "We want to play too."

Frank said, "Okay, you will be our reserves."

I expressed my joy, "We have a real team!"

BY THE SCRUFF OF MY NECK

Above is our original team before we had any coaches, and we only played pickup games against a few city kids, no Umpires. Left to right: Lyle, Floyd, Ronnie, Billy, Craig, Roy, Frank, Dewitt, Clinton, and Bobby. Other kids came and went over time, such as Jim Condon and Jim Galloway. Photo by Johanessen.

This always started great, and everyone had fun for a while. Without an umpire and with no adult coaches, things usually got out of control. There were always lots of arguments, and before long, there were fistfights. Jim Galloway was our first baseman for a couple of years before he summarily left the home. One opponent hit a ground ball to Floyd at second base, but Floyd bobbled the ball. And what should have been an easy out turned into a very close play. Naturally, the runner said he was safe, but Jim hollered, "No way, bub, you're out by a mile."

The runner shouted back, "I'm safe. My foot hit the bag before the ball hit your glove."

Jim said, "Oh no, I felt the ball in my glove before I heard your foot touch the bag." Then the runner went over and stood on first as if he were safe. Jim pushed him off the bag and said, "Go sit down before I knock you down." Within seconds, pushing and shoving turned into hitting and smashing.

Frank said, "Come on, we can't let these guys hit Jim around like that." Before long, it was an all-out fight with a couple of their teammates getting knocked out cold. That group never came back.

DR. CRAIG W. FISHER

To add insult to injury, we did not have the proper equipment, especially no catcher's glove or full chest protector. And a regular fielder's glove is not big and puffy like a catcher's mitt. And when Frank pitched, he threw fastballs that were always low and hard. By the end of a game, my hand would be hurting. There was an even more serious problem. The old half-size chest protector didn't protect everything. The chest protector should have a "tail" that hangs down between the catcher's legs, almost to the ground. Alternatively, the catcher could wear a protective cup inside his pants. Well, I had neither. In one game, Frank was pitching famously, and no one could get a hit off his low fastballs. But one of his fastballs came in just a little too low, hit the plate, and bounced up, hard-hitting me where there was no protection. A few minutes later, I woke up and found myself lying on my back with all the guys standing around me. I always thought that you had to get hit in the head to get knocked out. Then we continued playing.

In addition to just having the heart and determination to do it, Mr. John gave a lot of instruction on catching and batting. Once I told Mr. John, "I want to learn to be a switch hitter."

He said, "Ok, let's give it a try."

A few days later, after I batted left-handed a lot, he said, "Craig, I think you better stick to just hitting right-handed." I agreed and then asked if I could try pitching.

After one game, he said, "Craig, I think you should stick to catching. You're becoming a great catcher, and we need you there." I just smiled.

Mr. John worked with our whole team a lot. He immersed himself in our activities and seemed to enjoy them. He asked, "Would you guys like to play in a real baseball league?"

All the kids exclaimed, "Yeah, let's do it."

I asked, "What league? How do we do that?"

He said, "The city of Oswego has a recreation league, and I can sign you up for that."

He added, "I will try to get some new equipment for you. Craig, you need some catcher's stuff. Jim, you need a first baseman's glove. Most of you need new gloves and lots of baseballs." He finished with

"I don't want to catch any of you stealing equipment. If I'm in a store and see you carrying gloves and balls around, I will ask very loudly, 'Hey, what do you kids have there? Where are you going with all that equipment?'"

We had a discussion to pick a good name for our team. By an overwhelming vote, we named our team "Kat Walk Kids." Mr. John said, "Where did that name come from?" We explained how much time we spent running on the catwalks under the bridges over the Oswego River. He laughed and said, "Is there anything you guys won't do?" Nobody else in the home ever figured out why we picked that name. They thought it was because we try to walk stealthily like cats. We made our own uniforms, which consisted of blue tee shirts and ironed-on red letters "K W Kids" and red and blue hats.

This picture was taken of five players of our team shown above. Left to right: Ronnie, Craig, Frank, Floyd, and Lyle. The photo was taken by an unknown.

The league was organized by age groups, and we had to play in the section that accommodated our oldest kids. That means some of our smaller guys had a lot of trouble keeping up. We played in the league for a couple of years and did fairly well given the wide range in ages and sizes of our kids. We needed to use all our guys, even the youngest ones since the population of youngsters in the home started dropping downward. Importantly, I don't remember any more stealing except a few bases.

Our population, which was in the midtwenties when we first went into the home, dropped to under fifteen in the last two years. Little did we know that was a foreshadowing of the closing of the home.

CHAPTER 20

The Closing

I had just celebrated my thirteenth birthday last week on August 12. Now on Tuesday morning, in the third week of August, Mrs. Wyatt called me over and said, "You have an appointment in the visitors' room at eleven o'clock."

"Oh, I do? Is Pop coming?"

"No, it is a doctor who will be talking to everyone."

"What about? I'm not sick."

"Don't worry about it. Just go and answer his questions, and it'll be over in twenty minutes."

I sought out the other guys. "Hey, Floyd, did you hear about any doctor coming here? Did he talk to you?"

"Yeah, he's talking to everyone."

"What about? Are we going to be quarantined again? Remember how we were quarantined last year. I haven't heard about anybody getting scarlet fever this year."

Floyd elaborated, "I don't know why, but he asked a lot of personal questions. They were mostly about our friends and activities whom we got along with and whom we fought with the most. Was I angry at any of the caretakers?"

"That doesn't make much sense to me, but it sounds easy enough."

Well, my turn came, and the doctor asked several questions along the lines Floyd suggested. The doctor worked from a big black notebook. After he asked a question, he wrote a few notes in the book. Then the next question, he asked kind of a funny one that Floyd didn't tell me about.

"Do I know what a proverb is?"

I thought, *I know nouns and pronouns. I know verbs, so I probably knew proverbs.*" I wasn't too sure, but I said, "Yes."

Then he asked me, "What does it mean to say, 'A bird in the hand is worth two in a bush?'"

I thought, *What kind of crazy question is that?* After a long pause, I said what I thought was the obvious situation. "It is better to touch and hold something than to just look at it." Then he started to write a mile a minute. He wrote more about my answer to that question than to all the other questions put together.

None of the other guys knew anything about what was going on or what this was all about. The Monday night of the following week, Mrs. Reese, now the full-time director since Mrs. Dick retired, came into the dining room during supper to make an announcement. "The home is closing this weekend, and we have arranged for all of you to live somewhere else. You will either be going to a foster home or back to live with one or both of your parents or other relatives."

That evening, Mrs. Wyatt called us over one by one to tell us where we would be going. Frank and I would be going to my mother's apartment in Syracuse. Christine would be going to a foster home. Dennis, who had already left the home last year to live at first at a foster home and then with his mother, will be moving over to live with Pop. I said, "What about Frank and Ronnie? They are at Camp Hollis!"

She said, "We know, and it will be handled. Don't worry so much."

For more than four of our six years living at the home, twenty-five boys were living there. Seen below is the final picture taken of the last fifteen boys living at the home at closing time.

BY THE SCRUFF OF MY NECK

Left to right, top row (on the crossbar): Craig, Frank, Floyd, Ronnie, Bobby P. Middle row: Lyle, Richard, Dewitt, unknown on Dewitt's shoulders, Clinton. Front row: Johnny, unknown, Roy, Billy, Bobby M. The Photo was taken by John Johanessen.

On Friday, I was given a well-worn suitcase to hold my two changes of clothes, a pair of sneakers, a jacket, a hat, a toothpaste and toothbrush, and a couple of books. I asked, "What about my model collection?"

Mrs. Wyatt said, "You are such a worrywart. We will mail the models to your mother's apartment in Syracuse." I was going to ask more about Frank's stuff but thought I better leave well enough alone.

Sure enough, right after lunch, Mrs. Wyatt gave me a bus ticket to Syracuse and told me that when I get to Syracuse to just sit on a bench and wait for my mother to pick me up. After a long goodbye to the other guys, one of the maintenance men drove me to the bus station. I sat there for around forty-five minutes until I heard an announcement to board the Greyhound bus to Syracuse.

The bus was air-conditioned and had comfy seats. Even though it was only thirty-six miles, it was a pretty slow trip stopping at all kinds of make-shift bus stops in front of mom-and-pop grocery

DR. CRAIG W. FISHER

stores. Going through Fulton, New York, was quite nostalgic as I could see where our railroad tracks crossed through the town and where we rode our bikes through a park down to the Oswego River.

Finally, the bus pulled into Syracuse. I was overwhelmed at the size of the city which dwarfed Oswego. It was noisy with cars, trucks, and buses running all around the place. A park that was two city square blocks was surrounded by buildings, all of which were taller than the tallest building in Oswego.

It didn't look like much waiting was going on in the bus station waiting room. Many people were walking every which way and seemed to be in such a hurry. I found a spot on a long wooden bench and sat there with my suitcase. The clock said four o'clock. I didn't know for sure but guessed she probably worked to five and would meet me after that. Several women walked toward me and right by me for over an hour. One stopped, and I thought she was going to ask for directions or something. Instead, she asked, "Are you Craig?"

"Yes, are you Mom?"

CHAPTER 21

Syracuse at Mom's

Mom picked Frank up sometime Saturday afternoon. Frank told me, "Man! I was shocked when the Camp Hollis bus dropped Ronnie and me off at the home. It was eerie how dark and quiet everything was. I had no idea what happened. Then Mrs. Reese met us and said, 'The home is closed. You are both moving. Frank, you're going to your home in Syracuse. Ronnie, you are going to a foster home in Fulton.'"

Frank thought, *What the hell? I haven't had a home in Syracuse in around seven years, counting six years in the Oswego children's home and one year on the farm,* then said, "She gave Ronnie and me small suitcases, some clothes, and we had to grab a few other things. Then she drove us to the bus station and gave us our tickets."

Well, we started our two years living with her. Mom showed Frank to our bedroom and showed him where he can put his clothes. Frank asked me, "What do you think of this place?"

"Surprisingly nice. Look at all the rooms! Just you and I share this whole bedroom with a bunk bed and our very own dressers. The kitchen is big, along with the dining room and large living room. There is a real big couch, a couple of big chairs, and a TV!"

"Where does this side door go?"

"I don't know."

Then Mom joined in and said, "It goes to our backyard. You can play out there whenever you want."

97

DR. CRAIG W. FISHER

Frank and I both thought, *What? That tiny place? Nothing like we are used to.* Frank asked, "Where do we go to school?"

"Grant Junior High, which is only a half-mile up the road. I'll take you there Monday morning." She added, "There is a city bus system which can take you wherever you want to go. There's a bus stop right on our corner, and it went downtown. You can get a bus transfer and go to almost any place in the city."

She explained further, "Your father rented a single room in someone's home. Dennis slept in the bed, and Pop slept on the floor. They had modified kitchen privileges. They could use the kitchen only when no one else was home or everyone else went to bed."

We already knew about Tom living with Pop for about a year. That didn't work out too well, and Tom moved to Chicago to live with Aunt Bunny for a while. We knew Tom and Pop didn't get along, and we got worried about Dennis.

I asked Mom, "When did Dennis move to Pop's?"

"Several months ago."

"We thought Dennis went to live in a foster home in Fulton."

"Well, that didn't last long. In six months, he came to live with me. He was here for over a year until they called me and told me the home was closing. Your father and I talked about it, and Dennis moved over there to make room for you two here."

Frank asked, "What about Chris?"

Mom said, "She is in a foster home in Pulaski, New York."

"Can we go visit Pop and Dennis?" chimed in Frank.

"Yes, of course. Their place is way out on the east side of Syracuse while we're on the north side. You can go visit them by taking the bus downtown and transferring to the Fayette Street bus and getting off a few blocks past Columbus Avenue where we lived in that big yellow house many years ago." We found it to be a long ride to get there because the buses stop at almost every corner just to get downtown, and then we had to transfer to another bus to go way out east.

But with our background, it didn't take long for us to learn how to cut across town north to east on foot without going downtown at all. Frank said, "Craig, let's race over to Pop's."

BY THE SCRUFF OF MY NECK

"Yes, of course." We learned so many different ways to travel the 3.1 miles running on foot. Frank always won the races, but I loved doing it and planning new ways to go. We cut through parks, people's backyards, and old factory parking lots. Sometimes I wouldn't see Frank for many minutes. Then there he was halfway up the last hill. I tried to catch him, but as soon as I got close, he started running again.

I said, "Man, I can never catch you."

He replied, "You almost did. And if you kept running, you would have because I was so exhausted."

"Yeah, yeah, yeah, me too."

It didn't take us long to make lots of friends, and we became very active in sports. In Oswego, the YMCA had given all the boys in the home free memberships. And we went there as often as we could, usually a couple of times per week. We knew and loved the Young Men's Christian Association. We had played in a church basketball league in the Oswego YMCA, as well as on teams in the city recreation league. Besides playing on the home gym basketball court, Mr. John had taken us to see college basketball games. A few times he even brought players from the college team to the home to give us lessons and play with us. We loved basketball even more than baseball.

Frank said, "Let's go downtown and join the YMCA." We did but found out it would cost us quite a bit of money. We weren't used to that. But Mom and Pop both chipped in to give us a start with our memberships. At the Y, we asked about basketball leagues and found a church league. Then we met some guys from the Presbyterian church team. We said we used to play for the Presbyterian church in Oswego, so we joined that team with the caveat that we had to attend Sunday school regularly. There were other leagues also, but I think some seeds of the Bible and Christianity got planted in me during the Sunday school times. I liked the classes, the boys, the teacher, and the pastor.

Back at Mom's house, one afternoon, we chased her cat around the house with squirt guns. That cat was fast, but with the two of us, we usually got her good. Frank said, "She just went behind the couch."

"Okay, I'll get her here on this side."

"Good I'll watch under the couch to see if she comes running out." Sure enough, she did; and we chased her, breaking the coffee table in the process and leaving mud all over the couch and living room carpet.

The mud came from the backyard. There was a maple tree in the middle of the yard with a patch of green grass around it. Earlier Frank said, "Let's put a basketball hoop up on the tree." Soon the green grass was completely muddy. And after playing for an hour or two, so were we. We never thought anything of it and came into the house with our sneaks on. Mom shouted, "You guys aren't housebroken. Look what you did to the couch and table. Please leave the cat alone. And take your filthy shoes off. And always clean up after your selves."

Mom's habit of making friends with several different men continued our whole time there, which was about a year and a half. But there were some advantages to us. She often gave us money to go to the movies. One of the men took us to Syracuse University football games. We saw the great Jimmy Brown play the year Syracuse won the NCAA national championship. A few times, the men stayed over and got up and left early in the morning.

Frank got jobs at the Y. He worked during the school year and became a counselor at Day Camp Iroquois in the summer.

Frank asked, "Craig, are you interested in working at the camp?"

"Sure, I could use the money." He introduced me to the director of the camp. The director said, "All I can offer you is an unpaid job as CIT, which means counselor in training. After you turn fourteen, if there is an opening and you do well as a CIT, then we can offer you a job. Are you still interested?"

"Yes, I want to learn." I did well and became a regular counselor that year right after my birthday. As soon as Iroquois closed for the summer, we went out to the New York State Fairgrounds and applied for jobs. We sold newspapers, worked in hotdog stands, and did anything where we could make a buck. For twenty-five cents, you could

BY THE SCRUFF OF MY NECK

shoot two free throws; and if you made both, you win. Some ladies even gave me a few dollars to go and win large teddy bears and other stuffed animals. I could usually win for no more than fifty cents, and I pocket the $2 to $4 change. Frank and I began saving up most of the money we earned.

In the meantime, something went terribly bad for Dennis. We always knew he had trouble getting along with the other kids and withdrew from most of our outdoor games and hikes. But he had been friendly with a couple of the boys. He and Ronnie played a lot of games of chess and monopoly.

Earlier in life, Mom had told us that Dennis didn't speak right or relate well to others because he was deaf the first few years of his life. But now as a teenager, living in tough circumstances with Pop and going to a very large unsympathetic high school, he got into some real trouble. At school, several kids bullied him there, and we knew nothing about it. At the children's home, nobody bullied him with his two brothers around—especially Frank. Then one day, Dennis brought a knife to school and pulled it out when kids started bullying him. He was summarily taken away and spent the next fifteen years in a mental institution to be treated for paranoia and schizophrenia. Mom or Pop never talked about it. But Dennis told Frank and me.

Dennis blurted, "I tried to make friends, but all they did was tease me and make fun of me. I don't know why, they just did. Some even pushed me around. I ran away from them, but then everyone started calling me a chicken. So I decided to prove that they were the chickens, not me. I brought a kitchen knife to school and pulled it out at the first tormentor. He started running, and I hollered, 'You chicken or what?' Well, he went and got some teachers to come and protect him and stop me."

I asked, "Then what happened?"

"The teachers took me to see the school nurse who gave me a sedative. A little while later, two doctors came. After talking to me awhile, they said I need help, and they are sending me where I can get it."

Neither Mom nor Pop knew what happened. Dennis was living with Pop, but Pop worked in a factory all day. So he wasn't contacted right away. The new school didn't have Mom's work number.

Dennis continued, "They took me to Marcy State Mental Institution."

Frank asked, "How'd you feel about that?"

"I hated it. They told me that I was mentally ill and that electronic brain shock therapy would get me back to normal. But it was awful, so very painful. I couldn't stand it, and it didn't help."

One main impact on us was that Mom said, "Since your father has none of you living with him now, you both are moving over to live with him."

"What? That can't be. There's no room for us there," exclaimed Frank.

"It's already been decided."

Well, we went. For the next year, Frank and I shared the double bed while Pop slept on the floor. He gave us an allowance so we could buy hot lunches at school. After school, we usually walked downtown, drinking a quart of milk on the way. We spent the evenings at the Y until it closed at nine p.m. We also had to travel several miles to get to school as we did not want to start over in another new school. With very limited kitchen privileges and no way to take showers before going to school and no good place to fold up and take care of our clothes, the situation at Pop's became unbearable.

But another change, propelled by Frank and me, was coming.

CHAPTER 22

Syracuse at Pop's

"Hey, Frank, can't you stay on your side of the bed?"

"Whaddya mean? I just go to sleep."

"You're always bumping me or kicking me and taking all the blankets."

"Sorry about that. I can't help it when I'm sleeping."

"Okay, forget it. I think this place stinks. I can't sleep at night. I can't take those three miles to walk to school. And the buses take over forty-five minutes."

"Yeah, I agree. We've got to do something. Let's move."

"Where? How? Mom doesn't want us, and we can't afford it."

"Yeah, well, I heard that Mom is going to move to another apartment on the south side of town anyhow. I think she's going to get Chris out of the foster home too."

"Hey! That's great for Chris."

Then I continued, "Frank, do you have any ideas about us moving?"

"Let's start checking the apartments for rent in the newspaper and see what we can find, see what's available and get an idea of costs."

Over the next month, we read about twenty ads for apartments and looked at a half dozen of them. One was just right. It was an easy one-mile walk to school. It had three rooms plus a bathroom with a tub but no shower. We pooled our savings together and told the landlord we'd take it and paid the first month's rent. When Pop got home that night, we told him that we found an apartment, paid the first month's rent, and we were moving there. Pop just stood there, glancing his eyes back and forth between the two of us. His mouth dropped open while his shoulders seemed more slouched than ever. During that speechless pause, I added, "All three of us."

Then Pop said, "Okay."

The timing worked out well as Mom was getting ready to move and didn't want to move all of her furniture. Pop rented a van; and we picked up the bunk beds, bedding linens, the dining room table, a couple of dressers, and miscellaneous chairs and end tables. We even got some dishes, silverware, and pots and pans. We put the bunk beds and dining room table in one room. The dressers were side by side in a small hallway, and Pop slept on the floor in the front room. The kitchen had a sink, some cupboards, a refrigerator, and a small stove. After living in that one-room hellhole for the past eight months, this seemed like a mansion.

Pop went grocery shopping once or twice a month. Nothing ever spoiled on our shelves because all he bought were canned goods, jars of instant coffee, Tang, dry cereal, condensed milk, and cartons of ice cream. Sometimes he would take one of us to help carry the boxes of cans and even pick out some things. Cases of beefaroni, Chef Boyardee ravioli, and SpaghettiOs were high on our list. He taught us an easy way to cook that minimized cleanup tasks.

Pop said, "Just fill a pan half full of water on the stove and get it boiling. Then open a can of food and set the whole can right in the water. After a few minutes, the precooked food is hot. All you have to do is lift, with a potholder, the can out and eat the contents right out of the can. When you are done, throw the can away and rinse your spoon. No mess and no fuss."

We didn't mind that since Pop bought the food and paid the rent. And we could eat without washing any dishes. We did mind his constant lecturing us on the simplest of things. We never had a two-way conversation where our ideas, questions, or thoughts were listened to and responded to. Pop always just kept telling us stuff like vegetables are the best things to eat and never eat pork. To hear that

BY THE SCRUFF OF MY NECK

once in a while would be okay, but daily was over the top. He would also read about some animals and come out of his front room and explain all about them for a half hour and then go back to his room.

Pop drove Frank and me to visit Dennis in the mental hospital every two or three weeks. He always took us to fast-food restaurants like Carroll's and White Tower.

Pop said, "You can order whatever you want with one condition. That condition is that you all have to order the exact same thing."

I said, "Why is that? If I want something and the other two want something else, I obviously can't order whatever I want."

Pop responded, "This will teach you all how to compromise. And there will be no arguments after the food comes that someone got a better deal than the others. You all get the same."

"Grrr."

Pop professed to be an expert on everything. I continued going to the Presbyterian church by myself.

I asked, "Pop, why don't you go to church?"

He answered, "The pastors were on the right track, but I've studied it in more detail." Later Pop tried teaching mysticism to me. I ignored it. Also Pop said that he had the secret to winning World War II much earlier, but no one would listen to him.

Pop sure liked cats. We got a couple of our own, and Pop showed us that if we leave a window open, the cats will go outside and do their business. Then they will come back in to eat or sleep. We liked it because there were no litter boxes involved. The downside to this strategy was that other cats came home with our two cats. It was not unusual to have ten or eleven cats running around our already cramped three-room apartment. It got worse when a couple of females started having kittens. Pop didn't mind, but the landlord did.

The landlord said, "Either the cats go, or you go."

Pop had a great solution that would not go over well in today's world. Pop took boxes of cats and kittens to local playgrounds and parks and gave kittens or cats to young children to take home. If no one took the cats that day, he would just let them go free.

Somehow Pop bugged Frank a little more than me. It especially got to Frank when almost daily, Pop told Frank not to cross his legs because it was ruining the crease in his pants. I was a little more tolerant than Frank, which doesn't mean I was happier but just that I could eat crow a little better.

Still, he bugged me. When I turned fourteen, I had to get a birth certificate to prove I was old enough to work. Neither Mom nor Pop had one, so I went alone to Crouse Irving Hospital in downtown Syracuse and asked for one. The receptionist sent me to the records window. A chubby middle-aged woman greeted me and asked what I needed. After I explained, she asked my name and when I was born. I said, "August 12, 1943."

After searching some file drawers full of manila folders for ten minutes, she said, "We don't have one on that date for you."

"But you must. This is where I was born. I celebrated my birthday on August 12 for the past fourteen years."

She searched again and said, "Here's one dated August 13, 1943. Are your parents Ruth and Donald?"

"Yes." She made a copy, embossed it, and gave it to me, and I left.

Since Pop had a little chart up on the wall with all our birth dates, I confronted him. He explained that he must have made a mistake since my mother went into the hospital on Thursday, August 12. I was born in the wee hours of Friday the thirteenth. My brothers and I concluded that he was just superstitious about Friday the thirteenth.

Although we already knew how to play chess, Pop did teach us many chess tactics and opening strategies. He said, "If you want to improve your game, you should play over Grandmaster (GM) games regularly." This was good advice, but later in life, it disappointed me to learn that Syracuse had some great chess clubs and lots of tournaments which Pop never told us about.

I said to Frank, "Probably he didn't know about them."

Frank replied, "He knew about them but was afraid he'd get beat all the time."

BY THE SCRUFF OF MY NECK

Any GM today would tell a beginner to "play in many tournaments, record your moves, and replay your games over several times to understand your weaknesses." Pop wanted us to like chess. I'm glad I like it, but it bothered me as I realized much later in life that his strategy was to always break out half gallons of ice cream for us all to eat while we played. By association, we would have positive memories and feel good about chess. He treated us like Pavlov's dog. Everything was always calculated with him, not spontaneous.

To his credit, he visited us regularly in the children's home; but I later believed he considered it a duty, not a pleasure. There we sat in the visitors' room for precisely one hour, and then he went back to Syracuse. Now living in our own apartment with him in Syracuse, we found that he took no interest in our activities except to tell us how to do whatever better. When I made twenty-four out of twenty-five shots in the city/county free throw contest, he asked me, "What? Did you lose concentration? Why'd you miss that one?"

Generally, high school was great as we both made our circle of friends. And we did very well in sports. Our background in the children's home helped us become solid competitors. Frank and I played JV basketball together and took our team to the final game of the playoffs. Frank joined the track-and-field team and threw the discus and shot put farther than anyone else in the school. Frank suggested, "Craig, you should try out for the team."

"Okay, sounds good to me." As a sophomore with no training nor regular track shoes, I beat out a couple of juniors and seniors in the half-mile racing event. All of our running had paid off. A senior, Dominic, said to me in a back hallway, "So you think you are better than me. You better forget about it right now." I didn't even answer him while I heard him laughing behind me as I walked away. That year, our team won the city-county two-mile relay event for the first time. I was the first of four half-milers on our relay team and gave North High the lead which we never relinquished. Dominic didn't make the team.

"Hey, Frank, don't you think Pop has a lot of BO?"

Frank answers, "He sure does. Maybe we should tell him to take a bath once in a while." It was fortunate that Frank and I played sports and went to the YMCA every chance we could. We got hot showers five or six days a week. The next two years had some disappointments.

Going into our junior year, we were looking forward to playing varsity basketball and hopefully taking North High to the end-of-season playoffs. Frank and I were in the same homeroom class since he got held back in the fourth grade. He was more than smart enough, but while in the children's home, he skipped school so much the teachers had to hold him back a year.

One October morning, after going to our separate lockers, I went to the homeroom, but Frank was late.

The homeroom teacher, Mrs. Umbrecht, asked, "Craig, where is Frank? Is he sick?"

I replied. "Nah, he's at his locker and will be here in a minute."

Well, the bell rang, and we passed to classes without Frank. I didn't see him at lunch or after school. So I walked the two miles to the Y by myself. This is not unusual as many things could catch Frank's interest.

But when he didn't come home at night, it was alarming. Late that night, Aunt Bunny called and said that Frank is in Brooklyn. He wants to join the Navy, but they told him that at seventeen, he was too young and needed permission slips signed by his parents. Neither Mom nor Pop would sign. So Frank stayed with Bunny for a couple of weeks until he landed a job at the Y. He moved to the Y, and they gave him a free room and inexpensive meals. On his eighteenth birthday, he joined the Navy.

This was all very disturbing to me as we were the only two siblings that were together all of our lives to that point. It was not just me who missed Frank, but many school kids kept asking about him. He used to be "Big Fish" while I was "Little Fish."

As stated, Frank got away in October, moved to Brooklyn, and joined the Navy on his eighteenth birthday. Thus Frank missed our big Thanksgiving dinner. Pop came home from the factory carrying a turkey that the company gave out.

"Hey, Pop, that looks great! How are you going to cook it?"

He answered, "I'm not, you are."

BY THE SCRUFF OF MY NECK

"What, you know I never cooked one before."

"Well, I brought home a cookbook you can use. You can also call your mother if you need more help."

"Okay, I'll try."

I read the turkey section in the book and got started. But I skipped making stuffing. Also, I didn't know what truss meant. I didn't weigh it but thought it was medium size, so I estimated 15 lbs. and roasted it at 350 degrees for five hours. I brushed lots of butter on it every hour and started tasting it at the five-hour mark. I let it cook for six hours, and it came out pretty acceptable. We didn't know about carving and were happy to just take turns cutting off whatever we wanted. As I ate my first drumstick, I was as happy as could be.

I continued life under the scrutiny of Pop and little interaction with Mom. So I immersed myself in school, varsity sports, and the Y. Without Frank, our varsity basketball team went winless my junior year and 50–50 my senior year. While we had a poor record, I got some notoriety as a tie for high scorer for two years in a row. And I continued well on the track team.

Pop's degree of interest in my activities was zero. In those three years of sports, he never went to one game. Most of the other players had parents and family there regularly. He never went to any of the drama club plays I was in. He was not impressed that I was king of the senior prom. Pop also did not attend my high school graduation, my college graduation, or even my wedding.

While we always remembered that he visited us in the children's home, I never fully understood him. To me, he was a real enigma. I think he became a cross between a recluse and a stoic. He regularly told me, "It's not good to want something too much. If you do, then you can be disappointed. If you don't, then you will never be disappointed."

Well, I wanted something a lot, my own home.

CHAPTER 23

The Two Most Influential People in My Early Years

MR. JOHN

For the last 2.5 to 3 years of living in the children's home, Mr. Johanessen became our all-time favorite caretaker. He had such a long name, but he immediately smiled and said, "Call me Mr. John."

Mr. John immersed himself in our lives. Without being too maudlin, I'd like to summarize a few things Mr. John did. He came out in the fields to hike with us for miles down to and across the railroad tracks that carried coal to the coal barges at Port Oswego on Lake Ontario. After encouraging us to form a baseball team, he gave many pointers on how to improve. He took us to college basketball games at Oswego State Teachers College. He brought some basketball players from the college to visit us at the home. He took us swimming in Lake Ontario. He piled us in an old GMC truck and took us to drive-in movies. He taught us to play bridge and hearts. He brought his beautiful girlfriend to the home to play cards and visit with us. The list goes on, but mainly he treated us with respect and talked to us like we were real people. He became our hero. How could we not love Mr. John? It couldn't be just my imagination. He was real.

In January 2011, I searched the Internet and found Mr. John. After a couple of tries, we made contact. Mr. John invited Frank

BY THE SCRUFF OF MY NECK

and me to visit him in his new home in Florida. Over the next two months, we worked out a schedule for a visit to Mr. John. When we arrived at his home, we had nonstop conversation for the next six straight hours. It was so heartwarming that we all got choked up more than a few times. Frank and I kept telling Mr. John how much he meant to us and to our friends in the home. While he graciously accepted the point, he made his point that we all were important to him! That was a real shocker to me. Us? Important? He explained that as a youngster, he had plans to play pro basketball and did not care for school and did not plan on becoming a teacher. But a serious deep-sea diving accident changed all that for him. He had moved to Syracuse, New York, to play for a professional basketball team and start his dream of being a pro basketball player. Now he had to look for alternatives. He found Oswego State Teachers College with free tuition for future teachers and the Oswego County Children's Home for room and board. He found that he had a real aptitude for teaching and enjoyed caring for us. His life had changed forever, and we were at the center of it.

It is not by coincidence that Mr. Johanessen seemed like a hero to us. He was one. Mr. John Johanessen was a Navy SEAL, signed a pro basketball contract to play for Syracuse Nationals taxi squad, taught high school, started a high school martial arts league, and coached a team for many years. His teams won national and international titles. He was even a guest in the White House after his team won congressional-sponsored events. Some of his protégés went on to compete in the Olympics. He was an outstanding high school teacher for approximately thirty-five years. His former students and players write to him and visit him often. He is married to that beautiful woman Barbara whom he brought to the children's home to play cards with us all those years ago.

As our meeting in Florida began, I had some trepidation that perhaps he would just be polite and not remember us. The six hours of conversation almost put that to rest, but the clincher for me was something he said just as we were gathered in his front yard to leave. For a few moments, as Barbara, Frank, and I were talking, I gradually turned my head sideways and noticed Mr. John looking straight at me. I looked up at him, and he said, "You still have that same quirky little smile you always had."

Mr. John in the reading room at the Oswego County Children's Home in 1956. Photo taken by Craig Fisher.

Frank, Mr. John, and I in Mr. John's Florida home 2011. Photo taken by Barbara Johanessen.

Aunt Bunny

Miss Bernice Fisher, my father's sister, was our Aunt Bunny. She was the one person who made us feel truly loved. While my mother couldn't find a way to travel thirty-six miles from Syracuse to Oswego more than twice in six years, Aunt Bunny traveled hundreds of miles from Chicago, then St. Louis, and finally Brooklyn, New York, to see us once or twice a year. Her visits were the highlights of the year. She flew to Syracuse, and Pop drove her to Oswego. I remember the first visit as we walked into the visitors' conference room and she and Pop were sitting there. Instead of just sitting there, she stood up, spread her arms wide, and gave us all hugs. I couldn't stop smiling.

Then she turned to Pop and said, "Where do we usually go for the visit?"

Pop said, "Here, we only have an hour."

Aunt Bunny said, "I'll see about that," and walked out of the room. She went to the main office. She told Mrs. Dick, "Their father and I are taking the Fisher children out for a few hours, but we would be back before supper."

Mrs. Dick replied, "Okay, but don't be late, or they'll get no meal."

Aunt Bunny brought a couple of Chicago softballs which were bigger than a softball but smaller than a volleyball. We played catch on a bluff overlooking Lake Ontario. We laughed and joked around. She showed us an album she started called "Five Little Fishers and How They Grew." It had pictures of us as babies in our first home in Syracuse, several pictures of us at the farm, and she took many pictures that day and every visit after that. All of her visits were so much fun, and we still have DVD versions of the photo album today.

It was natural of us to sort of accept the visits without realizing what went into them. This was from about 1951 until about 1957, and she was totally occupied on her mission in life, the civil rights movement. In Chicago, she worked closely with James Farmer and George Houser to create the Committee of Racial Equality (CORE) in Chicago in 1942. Miss Fisher was a major influence in the development of CORE as a nonviolent force for civil rights. She became CORE's first national secretary. She introduced the "direct action" protest technique of the restaurant sit-in, in part modeled after Gandhi's use of nonviolent, direct-action techniques in India.

Miss Fisher inspired the St. Louis group to use the CORE nonviolent, direct-action techniques to accomplish multiracial use of various public facilities such as restaurants, diners, bathrooms, water facilities, drugstore lunch counters, department store eating facilities, and others. Just a few examples of success in St. Louis include the Chippewa drugstore (at Grand and Washington and at Grand and St. Louis); Sears, Roebuck and Co. (at N. Kings Highway at S. Grand); nine Walgreen drugstores; Greyhound bus terminal; East St. Louis bus terminal; YMCA at 1528 Locust and YWCA at 1411 Locust; municipal art museum; Fred Harvey Restaurant; and Schneithorst's Restaurant. Just five years after CORE began, these eating establishments were open to all.

The dedication page in the book *Victory Without Violence* reads: "To Bernice Fisher, whose voice sounded the call to action. And to the memory of the members of the St. Louis Committee of Racial Equality who pursued a quiet but determined crusade for human rights." Miss Fisher also served on the board of directors of the Brooklyn, New York, NAACP, 1960–1966.

After the children's home closed Frank, and I had many opportunities to visit her in Brooklyn, New York. She took us on civil rights marches in Washington DC, in 1958. She demonstrated and taught us to fight for the underdogs of the world. She helped organize unions, including working closely with Albert Shanker to start the Federation of Teachers Union in the 1960s.

In the early 1960s, she was on the executive committee of the Brooklyn, New York, NAACP and on the Steering Committee for the Concord Baptist Church in Bedford Stuyvesant, Brooklyn, New York.

Sadly, she passed away at the tender age of forty-nine.

CHAPTER 24

Epilogue

From 2012 to 2013, Frank and I searched the Internet via Google and Facebook to see if we could locate and contact some of the former wards of the children's home. It was difficult and time consuming, but we found six of the people who were in our ring of boys.

Unfortunately, there had been two deaths. My best friend Floyd and his brother Johnny died in their midforties. The rumor was that they were both drug related, but no concrete evidence was available. Their younger brother, Roy, became a quadriplegic and could not talk to us.

The next three yielded much more positive results. Lyle, my first boxing partner with the gloves, started out as a janitor in the Cayuga school district in the Finger Lakes not far from Oswego, New York. He worked there his whole post-children's-home life and became the chief of janitors for the district. I called him on the phone, and we talked for about fifteen minutes. He told me that he had a family and his children were all grown and successful adults with families of their own. He mentioned that his brother, Dewitt, moved to Florida, but they lost contact.

Billy Dickenson became a successful academic and is living well in California.

Boy Scout Ronnie, who blackened both of my eyes, went to a foster home in Fulton, New York—about twelve miles from Oswego. He worked as a technician in Nestlé's chocolate factory for about six years, then got fired. He moved to Florida, found a wife, and worked his entire career in a factory there. Frank ran into him at a chess tournament in Syracuse, and they had some brief contact before Ronnie moved to Florida. Ronnie still loved and played chess. Ronnie's older brother Clinton died of a heart attack in his midsixties.

The Lord must have been looking out for my family and me as we all had reasonably good lives considering where we started. Tom, after living with Pop for close to two years in that dingy one-rented room of Pop's made his break and moved to Chicago where he stayed with Aunt Bunny for a short time. Soon he obtained a job with a health provider and shot pool to earn extra cash on the side. He was not a hustler who sandbagged playing poorly and suckering someone into bigger bets. He told me that that would be a good way to get beat up badly. He became a regular at many of the bars on the southwest side of Chicago. He made a point of simply being there week after week on the payday of the guys working in the area.

After a couple of years, he met a lovely girl who was a nurse at the health organization where he worked, and they got married. While he loved and still shot some pool, he went on to get a job in business at Reflector Hardware and headed a customer service department. He excelled at that job and was sent to Kansas to start up a branch office there and eventually Portland, Oregon. After he and his first wife divorced, he remarried to Clare, and they have a wonderful thirty-nine-year relationship.

Given Dennis's mental illness, he had a much tougher life. However, he became an expert magician and put on many shows at places like the K of C, the Elks Club, various nursing homes, and many families for children's birthday parties and the like. He had a following and was in the local newspapers often. He married twice and now lives on his own in upstate New York.

Christine attended college and earned both a bachelor's degree and later a master's degree in psychology. She joined the women's branch of the Navy, then called the Waves. She saw much of the world and especially liked her station in Greece. Upon leaving the Waves, she began her career as a counselor. Her specialty, to which

BY THE SCRUFF OF MY NECK

she devoted most of her life, was helping hard-core convicts in state prisons.

Frank also had great success in journalism and photography as a career Navy man. He finished high school and a few years of college in the Navy and then achieved a master's degree in psychology and an ABD (all but dissertation) in psychology at Ball State University in Muncie, Indiana. ABD means he successfully completed all his courses and passed all the oral and written comprehensive examinations; these are major accomplishments. He held a variety of jobs counseling people with acquired disabilities who attended the Syracuse University (New York) assessment and evaluation of disabled persons in Rome Developmental Center (New York) and identification of matching jobs in the local communities for those individuals. Frank married a wonderful Icelandic woman named Gudny. Gudny was extremely active in establishing and maintaining relationships with family, extended family, and friends during their fifty-six-year marriage. Sadly, Frank passed away in August of 2021.

I did well throughout high school and college earning a BS in math education and then an MA in mathematics. I joined IBM and advanced through various midlevel management ranks and finally took a buyout and started a career as a professor at Marist College in Poughkeepsie, New York. The hard part was working on and completing my PhD in my late forties and early fifties.

Ginger and I met in college and married one year after college. We raised a family of three and had a good fifty-two years together. We were blessed with three children, who are now successful and happy adults. Unfortunately, cancer took Ginger away when she was only seventy-one years old.

I often think about the early days when Floyd and I discussed the Bible stories. Those stories taught me a lot. I say, "Thanks be to God for grabbing me by the scruff of my neck and pulling me out of a pit of despair."

DR. CRAIG W. FISHER

Oswego lighthouse. Source: Bert McConnell.

ABOUT THE AUTHOR

Dr. Craig W. Fisher, Marist College
Professor Emeritus, Information Systems

Personal web page: foxweb.marist.edu/users/craig.fisher

Degrees Held

BS: SUNY at Oswego, Mathematics Education, 1965
MS: Ball State University, Mathematics, 1968
PhD: SUNY at Albany, Information Science, 1999

Bio

Craig enjoyed a twenty-year career at IBM where he advanced through various information systems (IS) positions, from junior programmer up through IBM manager of World Wide IS Audit.

In 1989, Craig began a career as an information systems professor at Marist College, Poughkeepsie, New York. During his twenty-two years as a professor, he was program cochair and editor for the MIT 2002 Information Quality Conference and was president of the 2003 MIT International Conference on Information Quality. He also served on the conference board of directors for eight years. Craig is coeditor of a book titled *Information Quality* and is the lead author of the textbook *Introduction to Information Quality* (December 2011). He earned the SUNY Albany Distinguished Dissertation Award and produced twenty journal and conference papers.

Awards and Honors

- 2015 Best Paper Award, Information Systems Educators Conference (ISECON), Orlando, Florida
- International Association on Information and Data Quality (IAIDQ) 2014 Outstanding Achievement Award in Information and Data Quality
- 2011 named professor emeritus, Marist College
- 2006 Board of Trustees' Faculty Award for Distinguished Teaching, Marist College
- Faculty Recognition Award 2004–2005 for Distinguished Scholarship and Service, Marist College
- Distinguished Dissertation Award, 1999–2000, University at Albany, New York

Printed in the USA
CPSIA information can be obtained
at www.ICGtesting.com
LVHW041208241023
761966LV00003B/559